D0427121

## Other Works by F. Forrester Church

*Author*

Father & Son: A Personal Biography of Senator Frank Church of Idaho (1985)

The Devil & Dr. Church (1986)

Entertaining Angels (1987)

The Seven Deadly Virtues (1988)

Everyday Miracles (1988)

Our Chosen Faith [with John A. Buehrens] (1989)

*Editor*

Matthias Stele's Greek Wordbuilding [translated with John Hanson] (1977)

Continuities and Discontinuities in Church History [with Timothy George] (1978)

The Essential Tillich (1986)

The Macmillan Book of Earliest Christian Prayers [with Terrence A. Mulry] (1987)

The Macmillan Book of Earliest Christian Hymns [with Terrence A. Mulry] (1988)

The Macmillan Book of Earliest Christian Meditations [with Terrence A. Mulry] (1988)

One Prayer at a Time [with Terrence A. Mulry] (1989)

The Jefferson Bible [with Jaroslav Pelikan] (1989)

# God and Other Famous Liberals

RECLAIMING THE POLITICS OF AMERICA

F. Forrester Church

Simon & Schuster
New York London Toronto Sydney Tokyo Singapore

CAMAS PUBLIC LIBRARY

**Simon & Schuster**
Simon & Schuster Building
Rockefeller Center
1230 Avenue of the Americas
New York, New York 10020

Copyright © 1991 by F. Forrester Church

All rights reserved
including the right of reproduction
in whole or in part in any form.

SIMON & SCHUSTER and colophon are registered
trademarks of Simon & Schuster Inc.

Designed by Irving Perkins Associates, Inc.
Manufactured in the United States of America

1 3 5 7 9 10 8 6 4 2

Library of Congress Cataloging-in-Publication Data
is available.

ISBN 0-671-76120-X

*In memory of my father*

# *Contents*

# *Foreword*

I gave up on Bible, family, and flag twenty-five years ago. At the time, it seemed like the thing to do. As with most of my college friends, I had little use for organized religion; we knew our parents were responsible for almost everything that was wrong with us; and the American flag was flying over Saigon.

Today I am a minister, father, and patriot. Yet, over the years my beliefs haven't changed nearly as much as these shifting labels might suggest. The issues that arrested my attention in the 1960s—matters of justice and liberty—turned out to have a history. Without knowing it, I was following a path charted by my liberal American forebears, public leaders and private citizens who did cherish family, revere our nation's heritage, and draw inspiration from the Bible. I failed to claim this great tradition for two reasons: I rejected its symbols; and others stole them from me.

Much of my education at Stanford University took place in the streets, as my fellow students and I protested the Vietnam War and the university's involvement in war-related research. Those who supported expanding the war pinned little American flags to their lapels. Many of us took the bait, wore the same pin, and turned it upside down. Drawing from naval lore, we called this a distress signal, but that is not the message we sent. People who saw an American flag upside down didn't think of a ship whose captain was signaling for help. They saw irreverence and desecration.

Reinforcing this impression, some antiwar radicals went one step further: They burned our nation's flag. All of us continue to pay for this. Though flag-burning must be at the bottom of any law officer's list of predictable and dangerous crimes, self-proclaimed patriots are lobbying today for a constitutional amendment to protect the flag from fire. The real victim would be the First Amendment, which, by protecting freedom of speech, has long been the touchstone of our free society.

Looking back on my college days, the enormity of our mistake lay not in opposing the war but in ceding the symbol of patriotism to those who militantly favored it. Neither side possessed the whole truth. Extremists rarely do, and in our zeal we were often guilty of extremism. But many Vietnam War doves (including my father, Senator Frank Church of Idaho, a decorated World War II combat veteran) certainly had a right to the title of patriot.

One of my Stanford professors, Robert McAfee Brown, contributed to a book challenging our involvement in Vietnam. "We called the book *In the Name of America*," he wrote in a recent memoir. "We could have called it *In the Name of Decency*, or *In the Name of Judaeo-Christian Morality.* But we didn't. We were challenging what America was doing precisely 'in the name of America,' trying to point out that our own heritage had the resources to recall us from such folly, and that we were besmirching our name, our honor, our history, our sense of who at our best we feel ourselves to be."

The same holds true today. The fundamentalists don't own Jesus and the prophets any more than the Vietnam hawks owned the flag. When Jerry Falwell writes that God is in favor of "property ownership, competition, diligence, work, and acquisition," I wonder whether he and I are reading the same Bible: the one in which the last worker to arrive in the vineyard receives the same pay as the first; and the rich man is told to give away everything he has to the poor if he wants to go to heaven. As for the flag, I also wonder whether Oliver North and I are talking about the same country, when he (convicted felon or not) calls on us to "be faithful to those ideas and values that made this country what it is."

What ideas and values is he talking about? To be faithful to the things that made this country what it is we must embrace precisely what he rejected: the liberal spirit, its emblems an open heart, open hand, and open mind. However sincere, Jerry

Falwell and Oliver North win plaudits as patriots in large measure because the liberal tradition languishes in America, obscured in a thicket of rhetoric. No longer does the word *liberal* ring with the Liberty Bell or shine as it should from Lady Liberty's torch.

Of course, there are many good patriotic conservatives in this country. America thrives primarily because of the to and fro of conflicting viewpoints, often passionately held. We are sustained and advanced by the ongoing democratic dialogue. One starts to worry, however, when most of the strong voices, not on the fringes but in the broad center, begin sounding like one another. Reading the same polls, modulating their responses to the lowest common denominator, these voices beckon us tentatively but almost always in one direction, to the right. Hence this book, a patriotic essay, an old-fashioned "apologetic" for the forgotten rhetoric of liberalism.

Many of the people, texts, events, and shrines I visit will be familiar. My goal is not to break new ground but to hallow old. In reexamining the relationship between the American tradition and the liberal tradition, I shall focus on individuals and events central to our national self-image. George Washington, the Declaration of Independence, Abraham Lincoln, the Gettysburg Address figure in our history not only as historical figures and documents; like the flag they are patriotic symbols. Until they are reclaimed as also symbolic of the liberal spirit, that spirit will continue to languish.

My own liberalism, a family inheritance, is both political and religious. My political roots go back to my maternal grandfather, Chase Clark, a New Deal Idaho governor, and my father, Frank Church, who was elected to the United States Senate in 1956 at the age of thirty-two and served for twenty-four years. An early opponent of the Vietnam War and author of much of the principal environmental legislation of the 1960s and 1970s, he went on to chair investigations of the multinational corporations, the CIA, and the FBI. Following the footsteps of our founding fathers, he acted on his faith in America, not on his fear of America's enemies.

My religious roots run no less deeply through American soil—rich, various, and far more liberal (both in fruitfulness and essence) than sometimes it may seem. My first American forbear was Richard Church, a Puritan, who came to Boston with the John Winthrop party in 1630 and settled in Plymouth. Seven generations later, my great-grandfather and first namesake settled in Idaho. His son married a Catholic immigrant from Germany, and adopted her religion.

My mother's maternal grandfather, seeking a haven where he could freely choose his faith, came from Scotland, traveled across the country with Brigham Young, and became a Mormon bishop in Utah. My mother's father was a Quaker, as well as a governor and judge; he would never sit on a court case where there would be the possibility of capital punishment, because his religion would not permit him to pass this sentence. My maternal grandmother was a Presbyterian, the faith in which my mother and I were raised. I became a Unitarian Universalist as a doctoral student at Harvard, and for the past fourteen years have served as pastor of All Souls Church in New York City. Only in a liberal nation could so many faiths not only be protected but also nurtured and intertwined in a single family.

With liberalism in eclipse at home while emerging elsewhere throughout the world in so many unexpected places, I offer the following defense of the American tradition and my own personal heritage with a heightened sense of timeliness. Even this would have proved insufficient had I not received a generous gift of time from All Souls, permitting me to accept Dartmouth College's invitation to serve for two terms as Montgomery Fellow.

Special thanks to Kenneth and Harle Montgomery, who established this remarkable endowment at Dartmouth College; Assistant Provost Barbara Gerstner, who made my stay at Montgomery House as pleasant as could be; my research assistant, Michael Gildersleve; the accommodating staff of Baker Library; and my Dartmouth students, whose intellectual passion and rigor belie all contemporary stereotypes and give me renewed hope for our shared future.

Though none is responsible for any infelicities either of thought or expression, over the past year I have received generous helpings of advice from my editor, Elizabeth Anne Perle, then vice-president and publisher of Prentice Hall Press; my agent, Joy Harris; many good people at Simon & Schuster; and the following scholars and friends, who critiqued my work at various stages along the way: Stephen Bauman, Debra Berger, John Buehrens, William Sloane Coffin, Holland Hendrix, Carolyn Buck Luce, Louis Pojman, Toula Polygalaktos, Wendy Strothman, Donald Schriver, and Elizabeth Zintl.

I have been waiting for the right book to dedicate to my father, Frank Church. He was my finest teacher and closest friend. I miss him very much.

# Introduction

For forty-three years in the mid-nineteenth century, Henry Whitney Bellows filled the pulpit of All Souls Unitarian Church, where I now serve as minister. An imposing figure in liberal religious circles, he also helped Horace Mann found Antioch College, and organized the American Sanitary Commission, precursor of the Red Cross. This latter effort raised a then-staggering six million dollars to succor the wounded on both sides during the Civil War.

In 1872, he preached a sermon based on the St. James translation of a text from Isaiah (32:9): "The liberal deviseth liberal things and by liberal things he shall stand." By lifting up this text, Bellows celebrates the best of America, then and now.

> "The Liberal!"—we may thank Isaiah and his translators for that word; it is a good word, a brave word, a sacred word, . . . a name that ought to be peculiarly descriptive of the American patriot, the American thinker, the American Christian. . . . The founders, sustainers, propagandists of civil and religious liberty, should of course be liberals; that is, believers in liberty, lovers of liberty, devisers of liberal things—men of open views, high hopes, strong faith, broad charity, wide activity—large roundabout souls, loving and trusting the light; encouraging the freest inquiry; adopting the most courageous policy; interpreting constitution and Bible in the most generous way; allowing the most unqualified freedom of conscience.

Bellows was an evangelical liberal. So am I. People tell me this is an oxymoron. I don't agree. Evangelical and liberal are not antonyms, even in religion. Each embodies the good news, not the bad news of hell-fire and damnation, where women who have abortions are criminals, the wage of homosexuality is AIDS, and the homeless somehow deserve to be. Despite the prevailing notion that liberalism is both antipatriotic and antireligious, it is neither. God, the most famous liberal of all, has a bleeding heart that never stops. By broad definition, every good mother and father is a liberal. And the same can be said of our nation's founders and prophets. By defaming liberalism, right-wing Christians and self-styled patriots are unwitting traitors to the three things they claim to hold most dear: God, family, and the United States of America.

When the Carnegie Foundation asked Swedish economist and sociologist Gunnar Myrdal to do a study of America, he concluded that "America has had gifted conservative statesmen and national leaders. . . . But with few exceptions, only the liberals have gone down in history as national heroes." Small wonder, for as the dictionary reminds us, liberal means free: worthy of a free person (as opposed to servile); free in bestowing; bountiful, generous, open-hearted; free from narrow prejudice; open-minded, candid; free from bigotry or unreasonable prejudice in favor of traditional opinions or established institutions; open to the reception of new ideas or proposals of reform; and, of political opinions, favorable to legal or administrative reforms tending in the direction of freedom or democracy. Liberal means open-hearted, open-minded, and openhanded. This single word embraces the aspiration, both religious and political, of our forebears: freedom from bondage; freedom for opportunity; and freedom with responsibility, especially toward our neighbor, whose rights and security are just as precious as our own.

I fully recognize that many people who reject the liberal label, including any number of good conservatives, may possess most, perhaps even all of the above "liberal" qualities. When I speak of liberalism, I am thinking of public policy rather than personal attributes. For instance, Ronald Reagan is a generous, kind-hearted man, but in spirit and application the social policies he sponsored as president were neither. When he saw a hungry family featured on CBS news, he called Dan Rather to find out who they were so that the government could help them out. When Speaker Tip O'Neill told him of a single mother with five children who couldn't feed her family on the reduced food-stamp allotment, President Reagan asked his assistant to get right on the case, not concerning food stamps in general but this one family in particular. Each of these personal acts is a liberal gesture; neither led to a public act establishing a more liberal policy.

In the following pages, I shall examine the relationship between liberal policies and the American tradition, first with respect to religion, then politics, and finally family values. To understand and reclaim the liberal spirit, we must return to its sources and then adapt its message to contemporary conditions. As for the latter, developing those aspects of liberalism that are conducive to the building of community, I shall deemphasize certain familiar tenets that enhance the individual. Though this emphasis may differ from that of some contemporary liberals, to adapt the liberal spirit is not to betray it, for the liberal tradition contains its own regenerative capacity. Liberalism is not a fixed set of doctrines but a temper, a public spirit of openness and generosity.

Therefore, the term *neo-liberal*, much bandied about these days, is redundant, for all true liberals are in fact neo-liberals. Unwedded to any final set of policies, we are by definition flexible, open-minded, ready to adapt according to changing needs and realities. Governor Chester Bowles described the word correctly when he said, "Liberalism is an attitude. The chief characteristics of that attitude are human sympathy, a receptivity to change, and a scientific willingness to follow reason rather than any fixed idea."

So what went wrong? Why is liberalism in such disrepute these days? Perhaps the simplest explanation is that most Americans feel battered by the unfolding of recent history, and hunger for simpler times. After Vietnam, the King and two Kennedy assassinations, moral turbulence and ferment over civil rights, women's rights, and gay rights, many Americans long for something simpler—simple themes, simple messages, a Norman Rockwell portrait on the cover of a magazine. Conservatives seize on this longing. They promise a return to the dog by the hearth, its master dozing in a recliner, his wife bustling happily in the kitchen. They promise flags flying in the public square, and Americans proud again of their country.

I don't know what might have happened if liberals such as John Kennedy, Robert Kennedy, or Martin Luther King, Jr., had lived, but I do know this. Whatever their private flaws, each of them offered the American people hope and a vision for the future. Today that hope and vision almost exclusively come from the religious and political right, not from reformers who wish to create a more just society but from critics appalled by the consequences of social diversity and protectors who seek to maintain the status quo. That is one reason for the demise of liberalism.

Another has to do with semantics. The word *liberal* is a symbol. As with all symbols, we invest it with meanings that correspond to our experience. Depending on one's perspective, liberalism can represent generosity of spirit, an ethical approach to religion, freedom of speech and press, laissez-faire capitalism, fuzzy-headedness, profligacy, spinelessness, welfare statism, softness on communism.

Not surprisingly, in the 1970s and 1980s, when most of its connotations registered on the minus side of the ledger, when the rhetoric of public morality and compassion struck people as dysfunctional in the hardscrabble world of governing, the word *liberal* fell from fashion. It became the "L word," a word too tainted to be spoken aloud save in negative political advertisements. One might think of the demise of liberalism as a murder-suicide with only one victim, for many of the wounds were self-inflicted. As Lord Acton once said, "Every institution finally perishes by an excess of its own first principle."

Take tolerance, a liberal virtue if ever there was one. It is a noble virtue, but not always. In certain contexts to tolerate means to abide with repugnance. Yet some things are so repugnant that common decency demands that we condemn them. When the rights of criminals are more vigorously protected than those of their victims, or when freedom of speech extends to racial, religious, or sexual defamation, liberalism becomes an easy target, a self-caricature. In such instances, the open mind can be lampooned as an empty, unprincipled mind. Most disturbing of all, indiscriminate applications of tolerance invite a whiplash. When civil libertarians cannot draw a boundary line between license and liberty, those who lack sufficient respect for freedom of speech have a field day.

The same holds when generosity—the open heart and open hand—spills into profligacy. Contrary to recent punditry, Lyndon Johnson's Great Society did in fact sponsor several effective social programs, such as Head Start. But our inner cities did not benefit from undisciplined government giveaway programs. Paternalism proved a poor substitute for neighborliness. Compounding the damage, the liberal sponsorship of massive government intervention in such areas as school bussing and social engineering drove many middle-class and blue-collar constituencies into the unnatural embrace of the party of privilege.

Not only was liberalism razed by bankrupt liberal policies but out of the ruins rose the illusion that, left to our own devices, individual citizens and corporations would prove far more effective agents of charity and social service than had the previous generation of government planners. Not surprisingly, the free market failed to deliver. During the Reagan years the gap between rich and poor grew more dramatically than ever before. The rising tide may have lifted all yachts and battleships but the rowboats were swamped in its wake. Even so, much of the responsibility for this rests squarely on liberal shoulders. One excess invites another; that's how pendulums swing.

This is only half of the story, however. If liberalism fell from grace due to the excesses of some liberals, it also was pushed, a victim of adventitious right-wing rhetoric. During both the me-decade and the greed decade, liberalism proved an easy mark.

Here is where the liberal tradition, if made vital once again, can be so regenerative. There is nothing attractive about selfishness, about climbing up other people's backs to get to the top, for the welfare of each is to a significant degree dependent on the welfare of all. When we lose sight of this, when the spirit of compassion and cooperation is supplanted by that of unsentimental and cutthroat competition, among the spoils that go to the victor are the spoils of classism, sexism, and racism, each of which rots the foundations of the commonweal.

This continues into the 1990s. We have entered an era of tumultuous change. The world is shrinking; lines are shifting; comfortable boundaries are breaking down. Yet there will be no new world order without a new world ethic, an ethic of interdependence based on cooperation, not just competition, a *win/win* not *win/lose, both/and* not *either/or* ethic in which the good is not what one possesses but what one shares.

Here the liberal spirit, both religious and political, meets entrenched and growing resistance. For instance, since bunkers are fashionable in uncertain times, throughout the world religious fundamentalism has new appeal, as does anything that promises a refuge from contemporary reality. So does jingoism, the idolatry of nationalism. In each case, the accompanying rhetoric, playing on people's fears—of the other, the outsider, the stranger—is enormously effective, but the consequences are devastating. Victims of our own fears, we are in danger of losing our soul. If my understanding of the liberal tradition is correct, the soul we are losing is the soul of America.

To save that soul—though this may jerk the knee of many contemporary liberals—one must first remember that the liberal tradition of America is not merely a secular tradition. It flows along two streams that run parallel to one another and converge redemptively at critical moments in our nation's history. One is secular, but the other is decidedly religious.

From the outset, the American experiment was a religious venture, inspired by a search for freedom of belief and founded according to covenant, a religious agreement based on mutual trust, and not (like a contract) on law. The Protestants who first settled this country invested individuals with direct spiritual authority, to be supplemented but not supplanted by church law. Even before the Pilgrims shared their newfound religious freedom with settlers of differing theological views, the covenant principle, central to Puritan theology, established a basis for participation that led naturally to democracy and mitigated against hierarchy. Children of the Reformation, the Puritans emphasized the principle of private judgment. Casting into question the exclusive authority of religious hierarchies, they replaced it with a new and far more democratic principle: the priesthood and prophethood of all believers. By stressing the autonomy of the individual conscience, this opened one door to liberalism.

Enlightenment thinkers who fashioned our government opened the other door. It too had a religious key, shaped according to the law of nature and nature's God. In addition, underscoring the primacy of private judgment and conscience, our founders' insistence on separation of church and state complemented their Puritan forebears' spiritual aspirations.

In Europe, political modernization and democratization were unabashedly secular. Both met resistance from religious ideologues, who shared in the privileges granted by the monarchy and therefore remained faithful to the threatened ruling establishment. In contrast, our revolution was inspired by people of faith, individuals who, in the Declaration of Independence, appealed "to the Supreme Judge of the world for the Rectitude of our intentions," expressed "a firm reliance on the protection of Divine Providence," and drew from the religious tradition of natural law—today unnaturally feared by some liberals—to declare that all are "created equal and given certain inalienable rights." That liberty which benefits each and should therefore be possessed by all is nothing if not a religious idea.

Throughout our country's history these two liberal streams, secular and religious, flow in and out of one another's channels.

Abraham Lincoln regarded the Declaration of Independence as spiritually regenerative. Martin Luther King, Jr., drew both real and rhetorical inspiration from the "American proposition" that all people are created equal. Declaration signer Benjamin Rush, a Universalist from Pennsylvania, claimed that democracy "is a part of the truth of Christianity. It derives power from its true source. It teaches us to view our rulers in their true light. It abolishes the false glare which surrounds kingly government, and tends to promote the true happiness of all its members as well as of the whole world, for peace with everybody is the true interest of all republics." As described by American church historian Sidney Mead, "the theology of the republic" reverberates profoundly throughout our history.

To neglect the mutuality of the democratic and biblical spirit, especially as perceived by many of our nation's architects and social activists, is to strip American liberalism of its transformational power. In his book, *Under God*, Gary Wills says it well:

> Religion has been at the center of our major political crises, which are always moral crises—the supporting and opposing of wars, of slavery, of corporate power, of civil rights, of sexual codes, of "the West," of American separatism and claims to empire. If we neglect the religious element in all those struggles, we cannot even talk meaningfully to each other about things that affect us all.

Yet the moment our profoundly religious national character is acknowledged, certain civil libertarians, dogged in opposition to any hint of religion in the public square, profess their fear that the line of separation between church and state, prudently drawn and beneficial to both, will be blurred. If the American religious tradition is abandoned by liberals and left to the religious right, these fears may be justified. But this would be to cede both flag and Bible to those who reject the liberal impulse that informed both.

Besides, abdication is unnecessary. The surest protection

against an un-American co-option of government by religious sectarians continues to lie in the proclamation of biblical truths as understood by so many of our country's founders and prophets. From the outset, politics and religion have mixed in America, sometimes caustically, but often to profound effect. Their marriage gave birth to the liberal tradition. Only the renewal of their vows will keep it strong.

The key is community. The basic family values, civic and religious, that have helped to define our country at its best become central to any sustained renewal of the national spirit. For years these values have served within parochial communities to bring people together. Today, with the concept of neighborhood changing as rapidly as the globe is shrinking, a liberal family policy must take into account not only discreet families but as many members of the extended human family as can be accommodated. To help us find our way, there are blueprints in the Bible and the Declaration of Independence, and such symbols as the Liberty Bell and the Statue of Liberty. Nonetheless, the natural human tendency, honed over generations by the utility of tribalism, remains resistant to pluralism. Here we struggle with a new reality, for pluralism is emerging as the one essential ingredient for functional community in a global village. As Benjamin Franklin said—and never has it been more true—either we all hang together, or we will all hang separately. We even put it on our money. The American motto is *E pluribus unum*, out of many, one.

To help reclaim this spirit—America at its best—I shall begin with the Bible, turn to our nation's history, and close with the family. As both the noble and sorry chapters of our history remind us, God, country, and family will either thrive or languish together. That is the thesis of this book.

# I

# *Reclaiming the Bible*

I

# *The Most Famous Liberal of All*

And God saw that it was good.
—GENESIS 1:12

WHO IS THE MOST famous liberal of all time? It simply has to be God. No one is more generous, bounteous, or misunderstood. Not to mention profligate. Take a look at the creation. God is a lavish and indiscriminate host. There is too much of everything: creatures, cultures, languages, stars; more galaxies than we can count; more asteroids in the heavens than grains of sand on earth. Talk about self-indulgence, in the ark itself, if you take the story literally, there must have been a million pairs of insects. We may not like it, but that's the way it is.

Every word I can conjure for God is a synonym for liberal. God is munificent and openhanded. The creation is exuberant, lavish, even prodigal. As the ground of our being, God is ample and plenteous. As healer and comforter, God is charitable and benevolent. As our redeemer, God is generous and forgiving. And, as I said, God has a bleeding heart that simply never stops. Liberal images such as these spring from every page of creation's text. They also characterize the spirit, if not always the letter, of the Bible, which teaches us that God is love.

Admittedly, God's love is hard to approximate. To begin with, God created us in many colors; we come in many faiths, and two genders, with differing sexual preferences, a whole spectrum of political views, and widely varying tastes in food and dress. Such variety raises the level of difficulty as we try to live together in amity. It also requires that—created in the image of God—we cultivate the liberal spirit, especially as it enjoins open-mindedness and respect for those who differ from us, each a necessary virtue in our pluralistic world.

Though experience and observation lead me to describe God as a liberal, *liberal* is not a big enough word for God. God is more than liberal, much more generous and neighborly, far more imprudent than the wildest liberal on your block or mine. Most revealing of all, God's gift to us is beyond anything we deserve or could possibly have expected: the gift of life.

In the early middle ages, one school of mystical theologians, Dionysius principal among them, argued that, given the limitations of our knowledge and our vocabulary, the best way to describe God is by saying what God is not. Following Dionysius we can turn things around and say with great confidence that God is not *illiberal*. God is not miserly, parsimonious, penurious, or stingy. God is not narrow or rigid. Neither closefisted nor tightfisted, God is never spare when giving change.

*God is also not God's name*; God is *our* name for the highest power we can imagine. For some the highest imaginable power will be a petty and angry tribal baron ensconced high above the clouds on a golden throne, visiting punishment on all who don't believe in him. But for others, the highest power is love, goodness, justice, or the spirit of life itself. Each of us projects our limited experience on a cosmic screen in letters as big as our minds can fashion. For those whose vision is constricted—illiberal, narrow-minded people—this can have horrific consequences. But others respond to the munificence of creation with broad imagination and sympathy. Answering to the highest and best within and beyond, they draw lessons and fathom meaning so redemptive that surely it touches the divine.

Proposing that God is not God's name is anything but blasphemous. When Moses asks who he is talking to up there on Mount Sinai, the answer is not "God," but "I am who I am," or "I do what I do." That's what the word *Yahweh* means. When the Hebrews later insisted that it not be written out in full, they were guarding against idolatry: the worshiping of a part (in this case the word-symbol for God) in place of the whole (that toward which the word-symbol points). Politicians and theologians who claim that "God is on our side" often forget that "I am who I am" may have little to do with who *we* say God is. When we kill in the name of God, hate in the name of God, or justify an illiberal spirit in God's name, this is blasphemy.

Simply turn on the evening news. Somewhere in the world terrorists for truth and God are blowing up embassies, airplanes, and Planned Parenthood clinics. From Northern Ireland to the Middle East, God's self-proclaimed champions fight to the death, raising a gun in one hand and a Bible, the Koran, or some other holy book (perhaps written by Karl Marx or Chairman Mao) in the other. Many of our ancestors did the same, equipped with proof texts to drive home the point of their spears. Far too often war is synonymous with religious war: Catholic against Protestant; Shiite against Sunni; Muslim against Jew. Even the Greek gods chose sides.

Throughout history millions of people have killed or died in God's name. Religious passion is human passion writ large. When we care deeply, it is because we believe fiercely. This is especially true of religious belief. Our very salvation is at stake. In contests with underlying religious motivation, it is understood that we and our enemy cannot each be right. Too often what escapes us is that we both may be wrong. Religious wars of words can be equally ferocious. Spiritual leaders have long since perfected the rhetoric of bellicosity to damn their chosen adversaries. Even those right-wing Christians, Islamic warriors, and Jewish fundamentalists who don't go in for plastic explosives often enlist as soldiers for a fierce and vengeful God who damns more often than he saves, a hanging judge serving their own narrow interests.

When individuals without sympathy give the name God to the highest power they can imagine, their experience may construe this power to be as brutal as a wicked stepparent, imperious as an absolute monarch, strict as a boot-camp sergeant, wanton as an invading marauder. It is impossible for me to believe in such a God. Projecting my limited experience of the greatest concepts I know—love, goodness, generosity, kindness, and neighborliness—I see not a monarch (powerful, distant, judgmental, capricious, and controlling) but the spirit of love, working with us not against us, in a cooperative relationship, and for our common good. Reading both the tea leaves of creation and the high points of scripture, I can think of few adjectives that encompass the sweep, vitality, and heart implicit in both creation and the Bible as eloquently as does the word *liberal*.

People sometimes tell me they don't believe in God. I ask them to tell me a little about the God they don't believe in, because I probably don't believe in "him" either. I don't believe in the great father in the sky armed with a bolt of lightning aimed at the heart of his adversaries. I don't believe in a God that saves some people from airplane crashes, earthquakes, or hurricanes, while grinding others to dust under his merciless heel. I don't believe in a God who glibly chooses sides, and then brings in the heavy artillery. If the God they disbelieve in is anything like the God I disbelieve in, their God is too small.

Since our understanding of God is grounded in experiences of love and death, good and evil, peace and war, we cannot help but draw analogies from nature, history, and science in our attempt to approximate who or what God might be. We humans are not the animal with tools or the animal with language; we are the religious animal. Religion is our human response to the dual reality of being alive and having to die. When we discover we must die, we question what life means.

"Who are we? Where did we come from? Where are we going and why?"

These are religious questions. Children ask them. So do adults, when we can't avoid them. When a loved one dies, or we are given three months to live, the roof caves in on our carefully circumscribed existence. But there are other times when life, in all its awe-inspiring majesty, dazzles us and blows our roof away. In this two-chambered crucible of bewilderment and wonder our religion is forged.

So it was for the biblical Jacob, who wrestles for life and meaning with a mysterious heavenly messenger. Having struggled all night long, when dawn finally breaks Jacob demands to know his adversary's name. "Don't worry about my name," the angel replies. "It is completely unimportant. All that matters is that you held your own during a night of intense struggle. You will walk with a limp for the remainder of your days, but that is simply proof that in wrestling for meaning you did not retreat, but gave your all. Therefore, though my name is unimportant, I shall give *you* a new name, Israel, 'one who wrestled with both divinity and humanity, and prevailed.' "

Taking its clue from this encounter, liberal theology is grounded on the dual principles of humility and openness. Beginning with humility—and it may be a truism—the more we know of life and death and God, the greater our ignorance appears. Beyond every ridge lies another slope and beyond every promontory looms yet another vast and awesome range. However far we trek, while cursed (or blessed) with the knowledge of our own mortality, we shall never finally know the answer to the question *why*.

Today, two widely contrasting images of God compete for our religious affections. One, most clearly drawn by fundamentalists, whether Christian, Moslem, or Jewish, is a transcendent, all-powerful, and yet tightly controlling and judgmental God. The other, a liberal God, is both transcendent and immanent. This God is neither all-powerful nor particularly judgmental but rather co-creator with us, in intimate relationship, as we struggle together and suffer together in our common quest for growing love and justice. Those who have the former God in mind may find the very word *God* to be a fishbone in their throat. Others will struggle with a God more inclusive and yet, in a way, less powerful. The liberal God is not omnipotent. Children are hit by cars and die of cancer without divine sanction. The liberal God suffers with us when we suffer and fails with us when we fail, even as the life force or creative spirit works within us and others to make us better people and the world a better place.

The resulting image is that of a loving God, present in all, suffering and struggling with us in our attempts to be "kinder and gentler" people. Such a God is not an autocrat but a democrat; not judgmental but forgiving; not ideological but flexible. Such a God values cooperation over competition; relationship over hierarchy; peace over war; neighborliness over tribalism. Such a God doesn't divide people but helps to bring them together. And we come together by slowly recognizing that it is God's will to beat swords into plowshares, and spears into pruning hooks.

Religious liberals advocate respect for others not because we don't hold beliefs of our own but because we recognize limits to our knowledge. This has practical consequences. Mahatma Gandhi didn't advocate nonviolence to ensure the success of his cause. Nor was he seeking purity, though this too contributed to his motivation. The basis of his pacifism was far more humble. Fully willing to sacrifice for what he believed to be right, Gandhi could not justify harming another regardless of the cause, because he knew he might be wrong. Unwilling to impose suffering on behalf of error, he acted with vigor but not with violence, and the world was changed. His was not a wishy-washy position. It stemmed from a deep conviction, drawn from history and scripture, rising from deep belief in a liberal God.

Among Gandhi's mentors were Jesus and Henry David Thoreau. One of his followers was Martin Luther King, Jr. Each changed the world, not by imposing his truth on us but by demonstrating the intimate relationship of love and truth in his own life.

Liberals don't reject the old scriptural evidence; they reinterpret it according to new sightings, knowing from experience that both are rich with possibility. Religion has been a transformational force in this country precisely because at critical moments the "new world" spirit challenged the complacency and revitalized the prophetic vigor of our faith. Several of our most influential founding fathers—Washington, Jefferson, and Adams—were religious liberals. Respectful of the creator and creation, they freely used the minds that God had given them to interpret the nature of both.

None of them drew a more direct correlation between God's law and our own mandate to imitate that law in building an equitable society than Thomas Jefferson. In his preamble to the Declaration of Independence, it is God's will that requires the establishment of liberal values in any society drawn up according to a divine blueprint. Invoking "the laws of nature and nature's God" to confirm every people's entitlement to "a separate and equal station," Jefferson expands this notion of equality from a people, or nation, to all persons: "We hold these truths to be self-evident, that all men are created equal, that they are endowed by their Creator with certain unalienable rights, that among these are life, liberty, and the pursuit of happiness." America's egalitarian mandate reflects the liberality of the creator, and thus countermands, by divine witness, all feudal and aristocratic structures. It also parallels the Jewish concept of "repair the world," or *Tikkun ha'olam*, which holds that the human spirit is in partnership with God to help finish the work of creation.

This ethical impulse lies at the heart of liberal religion. It also taps into the marrow of the Bible. Jesus rejected the pieties of the local religious establishment. He followed a higher law, the law of God, which was expressed by the spirit of the scriptures rather than in their letter. The earliest followers of Jesus responded to the biblical literalists of their own day in like manner. The spirit of the scriptures gives life, Paul said; the letter kills. And James pointed out that works without faith may be dead, but faith without works is equally dangerous. It emperils our own life and the lives of our neighbors, whom Jesus calls us to love as we do ourselves. As Thomas Jefferson said, "It is in our lives and not our words that our religion must be read."

Being human and therefore limited, we cannot define God's nature, not finally, but the Bible helps. Created in God's image we are called upon to manifest the same spirit of love, generosity, and selflessness that inspired the patriarchs, prophets, and Jesus, whose stories fill the Bible's most telling pages. Judging from the spirit of the scriptures, wonderfully captured in legend and parable, God is not merely a liberal, but liberal with a capital L.

Given our penchant for literalism, to understand how and why these stories work, think of your own grandparents. For many of us, the stories we tell about them are a mixture of fact and truth, the latter an exaggerated or legendary version of the former. Stories drawn from their lives contain lessons that are more clear than the details themselves might suggest. From our grandparents' stories, we winnow lessons to help us become better people. They did the same, inspired by their grandparents' stories. Sometimes the facts get lost, yet truth is served.

I could tell you how my grandfather Clark lost his bid for reelection as governor because he let two hundred nonviolent prisoners free from the Idaho penitentiary, which in 1942 was rife with overcrowding; or how he sacrificed everything to move to Salt Lake City for six months when my grandmother was pregnant with my mother, to ensure that she would have good hospital care; or how, as a young Idaho lawyer, he bought new shoes for all his clients, so that they wouldn't catch cold in jail. Each of these stories is based on fact, but their truth has more to do with a combination of selective detail and distillation, which together make them memorable and moving.

If true of the stories we tell about people we know, what does this suggest about stories passed down from generation to generation, stories of distant ancestors, the heroes of our nation or our faith? They too are purified over time, unencumbered of incidental fact, focused for impact, distilled into truth.

Cynics dispute this. They argue that varnish must be stripped away so that we can see the cold, hard facts and be undeceived concerning our ancestors' and forebears' nobility. I don't completely disagree. It makes me feel a little less inadequate to know that my parents found a bottle of whiskey in my teetotaling grandfather's desk after he died. But I still pass on other stories of his life to my children, stories that over time have begun to develop legendary features. I do this because such stories inspire both my children and me to be better people and to lead more loving lives.

The same is true of the Bible. It too is a kind of family history, a treasure trove of stories passed down from generation to generation, distilled, revised, and improved over centuries until the stories finally were fixed into scripture. In presenting God's word and inviting us to divine and then imitate God's will, the biblical authors drew analogies from human experience that suggested the nature of divine reality.

For instance, the story of Abraham and Sarah attests directly to God's spirit, by providing a liberal mandate always to be generous and neighborly, especially to strangers. When Abraham and Sarah provided hospitality to three strangers, though they had little to offer, they opened their door, shared their bread, and provided shelter from the elements. As a result, despite Sarah's doubts and against all logic, this old man and his old wife parented a child, Isaac, the seed of Israel.

Interpreting this story, fundamentalists of the right insist that Sarah had a child when she was 100 years old. Fundamentalists of the left cite the scriptures of science to offer conclusive proof that this is laughable, impossible, an insult to the intelligence in defiance of nature's laws. Both miss the point. As many good people from Abraham's grandchildren's time until now have understood, the lesson spoken here—"Be kind to strangers"—has little to do with either fact or dogma. The story is about opening our hearts and homes to the other, the stranger, the homeless. It doesn't say, "Be kind to strangers because they may in fact be angels who give babies away as presents." It says, "Be kind to strangers because that is the right thing to do."

Put yourself in Abraham's or Sarah's shoes. Someone you have never seen before in your entire life, dressed in ragged clothes and ravaged by exposure to the elements, knocks on your door, asking for food and shelter. What would you do? Would you ask him in, add a plate to your table, and lay a bed for him?

I probably would not. Not that I'd slam the door in his face. Most likely I'd either send him to my church or some other nearby institution that offers meals for the homeless. Maybe I'd even offer him a ride. Not great, but I do know this. Doing whatever we can to make the world a little more hospitable is the most ancient of religious injunctions. Mindful of the story of Abraham and Sarah, my response is therefore bound to be far more liberal and generous-hearted than it otherwise might be. Perhaps the little I did offer in the way of hospitality might even invoke a "Praise God" from the man I tried to help. God is not God's name, but when we respond to the best that is in us, drawing from values passed down from ancient witnesses as well as kindly grandparents, God's image is present, and God should be praised.

In Jewish and Christian communities, the story of Abraham and Sarah, great-great-grandparents of us all, inspires us to be more generous people. Is this story factual? Perhaps not. Is it true? Absolutely, for it leads us to honor God's liberal spirit by being true to the best in ourselves.

I don't mean to suggest that the Bible is merely a moral playbook. Neither is God simply a human invention, designed to reflect our values or meet our need for an imaginary coach who will help us win the game of life. We don't only invent God; we also discover God. Looking at the creation, we strive to deduce the nature of the creator. We take familiar images of power and expand them until they become big enough to encompass the divine.

This is the stuff of legend, the raw material of myth. Fundamentalists, on both right and left, reject myth. One side embraces the Bible because its records are factual, not mythic. The other rejects it for being riddled with myth. In their quest for pat or rational answers to ultimate and finally unanswerable questions, they confuse truth with fact. Myth and parable are not restricted to the world of fact. They point toward greater truths than fact can begin to approximate. Even scientists, pressing the envelope of knowledge, speak of quarks and strings and big bangs; they too speak in metaphors.

The Bible is a library of sacred books which chronicle one people's search for and encounter with God. In addition to history, poetry, prophesy, and wisdom, it also tells the mythic story of life's beginning and consummation, as interpreted and reinterpreted by this people over time. By casting on heavenly waters their experience of the the greatest and most powerful things they knew, they caught a glimpse of the divine.

This has been true since the beginning of history. When we were cave dwellers, masters of fire, and hunters, God thundered from the heavens, electrified the landscape in lightning bursts of anger, and shook the earth. God also flushed game from the rocks into traps we set in the valleys below. When we were at the mercy of the elements, nature's vagaries, powers that threatened destruction or rewarded us by presenting food for our survival, God was there, a manifestation of the greatest forces we knew.

When we moved from a hunting and gathering to a farming economy, nature continued to reign, but the powers shifted to seasonal metaphors of planting and reaping. The female metaphor of fecundity supplanted that of the male hunter and spear-thrower. Sun and rain, sowing and gathering, birth and death: The rotation of seasons and the cultivation of crops were crucial to survival, and God became Goddess, whose womb was far more emblematic of creation and destruction than either lightning bolt or spear.

With growing centers of population and the transformation of villages into towns and then cities, a new model for power emerged. The king or lord who dispensed favors gathered a portion of each person's bounty, and led townspeople into battle against other kings and lords. Since our notion of God is a projection of human experience on a cosmic screen, each tribe began to view its own success and failure according to the divine strength and favor of its heavenly protector. For a time, each tribe had its champion, and human combat was resolved on a divine stage with heavenly protagonists stripping down and fighting for the human spoils of their devotees.

The next paradigm shift occurred when one tribe intuited that its God was everyone's God. Still Lord and warrior, with lesser enemies to conquer, the one God punished and rewarded us not according to our allegiance but according to our behavior. According to the scriptures, the God of the Hebrews even sent the Assyrian king, Cyrus, as an instrument of divine will, visiting punishment on his people when they failed to live up to his commandments. With the shift from polytheism to monotheism, destruction follows not upon the defeat of one's divine champion but as a result of his anger at his people's actions. This prompted the development of a religion based primarily on ethical foundations.

Once religion was personalized, with God rewarding our moral actions more swiftly than he did ritual sacrifices offered for his propitiation, new images, such as that of God as a stern but loving parent, began to emerge. "You are our Father," Isaiah said (63:16). Jesus spoke of God as "Abba" or Daddy. This sense of closeness finds even more intimate expression when Jesus suggests that God is not only beyond us but also within us, participating in our love for others and our quest for justice. No longer either victims or recipients of God's vagaries, with this shift in understanding we receive blessings according to our moral deserts and dispense them as agents of the holy spirit, the spirit of love and peace that moves among us and within us.

If myth is the projection of human experience on a divine

screen, parable is the discovery of the divine within the ordinary. The former is work of the mind, the latter that of the heart. When Jesus speaks of the Realm of God, he often begins his parables, "The Realm of God is like a man [or a woman] who. . . ." Perhaps a woman who kneads bread, or a man who buries treasure in a field. If made explicit by Jesus, this kind of identification can also be found in the Jewish tradition. Early in the Book of Genesis, when Abraham accepts God, God becomes part of his very name, which is changed from Abram (the people's father) to Abraham, or Sarai to Sarah (in each case, the "H" representing two of the letters of YHWH, the symbol for God).

In our encounters with others, but also with nature and art, we sometimes experience moments of peace and wholeness that reflect more eloquently than any theology the underlying basis of our relationship to the ground of our being. What the religious liberal knows, illiberal seekers, in their obsession with orthodoxy, often overlook: We are most likely to discover God when we allow our minds to follow our hearts. If God is love, which is as good a metaphor as any, then how we love measures our knowledge of God's true nature and our closeness to God more exactly than anything we may think or believe.

In sharp contrast, some theologians treat God as a cosmic butterfly, whom they capture, kill, and pin to a board for closer observation. Skeptics then point out that God is dead. However beautiful its wings, the concept just won't fly. Whether biblical or antibiblical, both groups are peopled by hard-bitten literalists, taxidermists of the creation, wholly lacking an eye for the poetry of God.

Think of the creation as a masterpiece, the most highly nuanced and unfathomable masterpiece of all. As with any great work of art, interpretations concerning its meaning will differ. The greater the work, the more spirited and contentious the debate will be. This is certainly true of religion, where the task, in large measure, is to ponder the creation and make sense of it.

To understand religious passions, one can strike an analogy

between competing schools of religious interpretation and those fierce little conventicles of literary critics who people our academies. For instance, while *Moby Dick* is acknowledged by many as a masterpiece, perhaps the greatest work of American literature, there are a myriad of interpretations: symbolist, Marxist, existentialist, deconstructionist, Jungian, Freudian, and structuralist, to name only a few.

During Henry Whitney Bellows's time, Herman Melville was an occasional member of the congregation I now serve. (A far more stuffy and successful writer, William Cullen Bryant, served on the board of trustees and occupied a front pew.) Several times, Melville's wife met with Dr. Bellows to discuss her marital difficulties, but Melville himself was decidedly a reluctant back bencher.

One day, hoping to help illuminate the theology in *Moby Dick*, some enterprising Melville scholar will immerse herself in Bellows's sermons. She'll probably even learn a little something. Then she'll write a highly detailed monograph. However brilliant, neither this one nor any other interpretation of *Moby Dick* will ever be complete. The book is far too rich and vast even for any cluster of interpretations to comprehend its meaning.

If *Moby Dick* and other masterpieces continue to resist final explication, it is hardly surprising that the creation, the greatest and most impenetrable masterpiece of all, should prove a far more thorny text. Rifling through Bellows's sermons may teach us little about Melville's theology, but the same exercise would teach us even less about God. Bellows was one of the finest, most thoughtful, and profoundly Christian preachers of his day, but like every other preacher, regardless of theological stripe or mental gift, he too was outmastered by the overwhelming nature of the task.

When interpreting any creative work, whether a novel or the cosmos itself, the difficulty of the task rises with the intellectual and emotional complexity of the text. When the text is the creation—especially given that we are a part of what we are trying to interpret—an almost unfathomable level of difficulty is further compounded by the anxiety implicit in such questions as "How can I be saved?"

People with differing interpretations of *Moby Dick* may disagree with one another in print, but their arguments are nothing when compared to how those with differing interpretations of the creation act when facing off in the religious arena. A handful of literary critics may believe that their interpretation of a masterpiece alone is correct, but, when it comes to God, many, if not most, believers insist on the absolute truth of their opinion.

Their logic is as follows: If A (my belief) is correct, not-A (everyone else's) has to be wrong. In circles where right thinking takes precedence over right acting, when advocates of one particular dogma are confronted by others who disagree, they must either convert, ignore, or destroy them. Hence the long history of religious war and persecution.

How much better it would be if we thought of the world as a cathedral, with thousands of different windows through which the light of God or truth shines. Some are abstract, some representational. Each tells a story about what it means to be alive and then to die, a story of love and death, hope and faith, truth and meaning.

Some people think that the light shines only through their own window. Fundamentalists of the right, sure that their window is the only one through which the light shines, may go so far as to incite their fellow worshipers to throw stones through other people's windows. Atheists, fundamentalists of the left, observe the bewildering variety of windows and lapse into skepticism, concluding that there is no light. But the windows are not the light, only where the light shines through. There is one light (one truth, one God), but it is refracted through a myriad of windows, each distinct, each different.

Those who have worshiped at one window throughout their lifetime almost always see the refracted light more clearly and understand its meaning more deeply than do those who flit from window to window, believing that differences don't really matter. In religion, the discipline that comes from devotion cannot be replaced by sophistication. But in a pluralistic world, the best we can still hope for is the development of deep commitments to our own faith, while somehow remaining able to acknowledge that those who believe differently may, in their own distinctive ways, be just as close to God or truth as we are. Then we may live as neighbors in the cathedral of the world.

That is the liberal hope, as inspired by two great commandments: to love God and our neighbor as ourself.

# 2

# *God's Son Jesus*

Truly I say to you, as you did it unto one of the least of these, you did it unto me.

—MATTHEW 25:40

IF GOD IS THE most famous liberal of all time, his son Jesus surely comes in a close second. It is not a question of sweetness and light. Jesus was often angry. He turned over the tables of the money changers. He scorned the religious establishment of his own day, branding them as liars and hypocrites.

Jesus's liberalism was founded on two principles that always distinguish religious liberals from their more traditional contemporaries: He was not a biblical literalist, and he disdained every superficial form of religious show, whether moralism, pietism, or doctrinal presumption. Jesus placed the burden of religious proof not in saving words but in saving works.

Both principles are important, and each is ignored by the more vocal and insistent of Jesus's so-called followers. In many Christian circles, biblical literalism is the key to salvation, and private, rather than public, morality is a litmus test of one's Christian sincerity. Nothing could less honor the memory of a man who so eloquently challenged the religious presumptions of his time. In contrast with the Pharisees, those good people who were the biblical literalists and moralists of their day, Jesus sought a far deeper proof of faith, one ratified by deeds not words. He was unimpressed by propriety and fearless in his advocacy of society's lost sheep: outcasts, untouchables, all the forgotten ones.

As for his disdain of biblical literalism, consider the sabbath law, duly codified in scripture. Proclaiming that "The sabbath was made for man, not man for the sabbath," Jesus aligned himself with the spirit, not the letter, of the Bible. Those who wish to enact Christian laws in our own country must beware. The person in whose name they are acting would have cringed at the very thought.

Preachers on the far religious right have long lamented that we have abandoned the faith of our founders. Their argument goes as follows: The architects of the Revolution, Declaration of Independence, and Constitution were Christians, whose intention—to establish the United States as a Christian nation founded on Christian laws—was so obvious that they didn't bother making it explicit.

They could not be more wrong.

Consider this long-forgotten anecdote, a brush between the protectors of Christian law and the father of our country. On a Sunday morning in December, 1789, eleven months after his election to the presidency, George Washington was arrested on his way to church. According to a report in the December 16 *Massachusetts Centinel*, Washington had lost his way riding through Connecticut and was unable to reach New York State on Saturday night as planned. Having agreed to attend worship in New York the next morning, he awakened early, mounted his horse, and took off at a fast clip toward the New York–Connecticut border.

What Washington neglected to consider—or chose to overlook—was that riding at full speed in Connecticut on a Sunday was against the law. Before he had crossed the border, an alert tithingman halted the president, and cited him for violating the local sabbath statutes. This obscure incident marks the first (if least momentous) time that anyone rightfully accused our president of breaking the law.

Among the earliest laws to be established in colonial America, Christian sabbath statutes concerned everything from a requirement to attend church twice every Sunday (Virginia, 1610) to bans on Sunday labor (Massachusetts Bay, 1629), unnecessary travel (Plymouth, 1682), and drinking on Sunday (New Jersey, 1701). Penalties ranged from ten shillings or a whipping to a fine of fifty pounds of tobacco.

The secondary player in this minor drama was a tithingman, whose task it was to ensure that all Sabbath legislation be properly observed and rigorously enforced. In addition to people traveling unnecessarily or too fast on a Sunday, the tithingman also kept tabs on all those "who lye at home," and apprehended anyone who "prophanely behaved, lingered without dores at meeting time on the Lordes daie," which included those "sons of Belial strutting about, setting on fences, and otherwise desecrating the day." In addition to fines and whippings, in most states the favored penalties also ensured public embarrassment. As "good" (law-abiding) Christians walked to and from church, their guilty neighbors—whether Sunday travelers, speedsters, revelers, blasphemers, or sleepers—found themselves on display in a cage right in front of the church on the meeting-house green.

As a clergyman in Manhattan, the secular mecca of America, I am tantalized by the vision of all my neighbors who prop themselves up in bed and devote Sunday morning to consuming coffee and the *New York Times* being mustered out by the local constabulary and caged in Central Park. Of course, being modern white-collar (or silk-pajama) criminals, the punishment would be far less stiff than in the good old days, when America was a truly Christian country. Just imagine. The Tavern on the Green could cater. Wouldn't it be grand.

The real irony in this story is that when President Washington was arrested for breaking the Sabbath he was on his way to church. He did manage to talk himself out of trouble, and made it to services on time, but only when he promised to travel no further that day than the town where he planned to worship. Nonetheless, Washington was nearly thwarted by a Christian law from performing his Christian duty. This is because, almost by definition, any piece of Christian legislation—not Christian in spirit, such as a law to aid the hungry or homeless, but one drafted to enforce specific religious behavior or practice—runs counter to the teachings of Jesus.

Following the precedent of the great Rabbi Hillel (who taught that the sabbath commandment was secondary to the commandment to be hospitable to one's neighbor), when confronted by a man in need of healing on the Sabbath, Jesus didn't give the law a second thought. Choosing to serve God, rather than God's blindered bureaucrats, he broke the Sabbath ordinance, and healed the man. For this, the strict-to-the-letter religious authorities called him before their tribunal and accused him of sacrilege.

In seventeenth- or eighteenth-century New England, should anyone have wished to attempt a like bit of timely healing on the Sabbath day, he or she too might have been thwarted by the local (now dogmatic Christian) authorities. The tithingman did hand out tickets, giving special permission to those who could be excused from the Sunday statutes by virtue of some emergency. But imagine if one of your children were to fall deathly ill on a Sunday. To follow the letter of the law, before you could travel to the doctor's home to enlist professional aid, first you would have to find the tithingman and secure his permission. However well-intentioned, this statute, written to defend Christianity from bad Christians and other reprobates, potentially makes it impossible to be a good Christian, a healer, a follower of Jesus.

For years, Jesus has been held captive by people who claim to believe in him. But his own words persist, defying their deed of ownership. Jesus was no conservative. He challenged the establishment, both religious and political. Would anyone who turned over the money-changers' tables in the temple have had anything nice to say about today's televangelists? Of course not. And what about those who pride themselves for saving the taxpayers' money by slashing social programs. Not Jesus. He had no use for pride, and always came down on the side of the dispossessed and downtrodden: prostitutes, prodigal children, tavern keepers, even tax collectors.

The Bible can be quoted by anyone for his or her own purposes. In its pages, there are passing references to the evils of everything from women to shellfish. But far from being a biblical literalist, Jesus himself drew a sharp distinction between the transient and permanent teachings contained in the scriptures. When brought before the religious authorities and charged with breaking sacred laws, Jesus summed up the Hebrew scriptures in two great commandments, which override all lesser particulars: "You shall love the Lord your God with all your heart, and with all your soul, and with all your might. This is the great and first commandment. And a second is like it, You shall love your neighbor as yourself. On these two commandments," he said, "depend all the law and the prophets" (Matthew 22). Again, Jesus follows in the spirit of Hillel, who wrote, "What is hateful to you, do not to your neighbor. That is the Torah. All the rest is commentary."

If the word *liberal* means generous (washing his disciples' feet), indulgent (allowing his own to be bathed in costly oils), compassionate (taking pity on the forgotten members of society), flexible and nondoctrinaire (breaking the sabbath laws to serve a person in need), and free-spirited (dancing and drinking, honoring the spirit of the law above its letter), Jesus was a quintessential liberal.

Of course, the word *liberal* alone is insufficient to encompass either Jesus's person or teachings. Jesus himself asked, "Who do people say that I am?" His disciples, who themselves were far from sure, replied, "John the Baptist," "Elijah," "one of the prophets," perhaps "the messiah." The gospels are filled with clues, though many were written long after Jesus died by followers convinced that he was the long-awaited scion of David, God's only son come to proclaim salvation and pronounce judgment. One sign of Jesus's greatness and importance is that we continue to struggle in our attempts to understand who he was and what, precisely, his message portends.

Throughout the centuries, Christian theologians and religious scholars have struggled with the question Jesus asked his disciples. The search for the historical Jesus has led sincere seekers down many different paths. Was Jesus a revolutionary zealot or a pacifist? Was he a man, a God, or both? Was he an apocalypticist, who believed that the end of the world would come during his disciples' lifetime as he says to them in Matthew 10:23, or a social prophet whose ethical teachings were offered for the reform of society? Depending on one's answer to these and other like questions, Jesus appears in many different lights, each to a degree illuminating but none sufficient to highlight his entire character or message.

When I speak of Jesus as a liberal, I limit myself to his teachings, not teachings about him. Even here, his proclamations of unconditional love and forgiveness contrast with others that are judgmental. Yet, I can say this. When we extract those fragments of his gospel that Jesus himself underlines as having precedence and ultimacy, we encounter a man for whom deeds are superior to creeds, and service to the poor and downtrodden is the key to salvation.

In some respects, Jesus is more than liberal, in fact nothing less than radical. Those who enlist Jesus as chairman of the cosmic board, a hard-working, no-nonsense free-market capitalist, ought to go back and ponder the story of the rich man who wishes to know how he can ensure himself a place in heaven. The answer is not drawn from the book of supply-side or trickle-down economics. It is not "Make as much money as possible, so that your tithe to the church will grow yearly, and you will collect dividends in heaven." What Jesus actually said is "Take all you have and give it to the poor."

Three years ago, one of my parishioners confronted me with this passage. A world-beating Wall Street whiz-kid, Bart Harvey had begun to question what the fast track meant. Looking for deeper meaning out of life, he came into my study and said, "I've been reading the Bible. I'm thinking of giving everything I have to the poor. I know it sounds crazy, but according to Jesus, it's the only way I can be saved."

He happened to be one of my leading parishioners: a major giver; treasurer of the board; young, handsome; a vital and important member of our church. I remember how pleased I was when he joined All Souls. He was appealing, generous and, unlike the majority of our members, very well off.

"You are doing so much already," I said. "By tithing here, through your support of our social ministries and other social programs, you are giving as much to the poor as almost anyone I know." He didn't buy it. Instead, he quit his job, went mountain climbing in Nepal, and spent several weeks walking through India. When he returned to New York, his brokerage firm offered him his old job back, with a major raise. Bart turned down the offer, choosing instead to assist James Rouse (the developer of Columbia, Maryland, Faneuil Hall Marketplace in Boston, and the South Street Seaport in New York), who now devotes his creative efforts to facilitate housing for the poor. Had it not been for Bart's lobbying efforts, Congress would likely have canceled the tax credit program that makes much private-sector low-cost housing possible. Fortunately, when I told him that he didn't need to take Jesus seriously, Bart didn't listen to me.

He came back to see me recently. Two things struck me about him. First, he was doing more good than almost anyone I know. Second, he had lost his need to be virtuous, better than his neighbors. As he grew in service, Bart also grew in humility. Jesus would have understood that also.

In contrast, many Christians today reject the notion that Jesus espoused a radical economic gospel. They overlook his parable concerning the laborers in the field. At the outset of the day a group of laborers are offered a set fee for twelve hours of work. At midday others come to work in the field, and sign on for the same fee. A few stragglers arrive just before closing time. Are they paid proportionately? Not at all. In fact, they pocket exactly the same wage given to those who had been slaving in the field from dawn until dusk.

As with many of Jesus's parables, this one is designed to shock, breaking his listeners' expectations so that we will awaken to a new appreciation for the bounteousness of God. He reminds us that those who find faith late in the day are as worthy as those who have long worked in the proverbial vineyards. Jesus is not really talking economics here. Yet he is demonstrating by means of a parable that God is far more generous, accommodating, and bounteous with those who turn to him than is any local businessman with his employees or payroll.

A similar message lies at the heart of Jesus's parable of the Prodigal Son. This story is really about two sons and their liberal father. Throughout his entire life, one son has been the model of propriety and rectitude: saving his inheritance, obeying his parents, eschewing immorality, working hard, following the letter of the law. The other son takes his inheritance and squanders it: whoring and gaming, lying and stealing, living a life of riot and self-indulgence, until he manages to dissipate not only himself but all the money his father has given him. At the end of his pleasure trip, broke and broken, the prodigal returns home, expecting to be punished, perhaps even banished by his father. Instead, the old man runs out to meet him at the gate, embraces him, and cries tears of joy at this unexpected reunion. Rushing back to the house he instructs his servants to go out and slaughter a calf, an enormous luxury.

Put yourself in the dutiful son's shoes. He has been the perfect son, yet his father never cried tears of joy over him. Besides, the calf could have been sold at market for a good price, not to mention that they were sacrificing this promised income for his wastrel of a brother who went out and broke every moral law: Honor thy father and mother; thou shalt not steal; thou shalt not covet another's property; thou shalt not commit adultery. By nightfall this scoundrel is seated in the place of honor, on their father's right hand, at their hallowed family table, which shortly before he had desecrated by his absence, disobedience, and folly.

No parable could be more liberal in spirit. Not only is generosity golden but those who think by virtue of their piety, education, or wealth that they are more deserving than other people are in for a surprise. According to Jesus, the Commonwealth of God is an egalitarian realm. Entrance is secured not by hard work, proper behavior, public religious observance, or even by strict morality. The only key to the Kingdom is a contrite and loving heart.

Even right theology doesn't matter. Take the passage in Matthew 25 where Jesus tells his disciples that when we die there is a quiz. The questions are not "Who is the second person in the trinity?" or "Should women be allowed to be priests?" or "During your lifetime were you sufficiently militant in your abhorrence of communism, homosexuality, and abortion?" They are "Did you feed the hungry; clothe the naked; heal the sick; visit those in prison?" If you get the answers correct, you go to heaven.

In his injunction to care for the distressed and downtrodden—"because whenever you do unto the least of these, you do unto me"—Jesus follows in the prophetic tradition of Isaiah, who said that our religious charge is "to loose the bands of wickedness, to undo the thongs of the yoke, to let the oppressed go free, and to break every yoke . . . to share your bread with the hungry, and bring the homeless poor into your house; when you see the naked, to cover him, . . . [for] If you pour yourself out for the hungry and satisfy the desire of the afflicted, then shall your light rise in the darkness, and your gloom be as the noonday." That is the essence of the liberal gospel.

By definition, every religious establishment is conservative. Its object, by no means an ignoble one, is to uphold traditions, maintain customs, and preserve order. Yet, apart from the two great commandments, there are no religious laws mandating love, only laws prescribing and proscribing moral and ritual behavior. This is why we need prophets, men and women who arise among the people, to proclaim that the religious establishment, the priests and teachers, are so busy enforcing their religious laws and rules that they have lost sight of God's law, the law of love being shared and justice done.

Whoever and whatever else he may have been, Jesus was

clearly such a prophet. Upon hearing the noble words of Isaiah intoned by temple authorities as holy scripture, he could not have helped but observe that these same radical teachings were not being honored. On the contrary, the spirit of love and justice proclaimed by the prophets (who cursed the religious authorities of their own day) were being smothered by legalism, pietism, and moralism.

When wearing his prophetic mantle, whether overturning the money-changers' tables or prophesying the certain destruction of the "liars and hypocrites" who preached and taught there, Jesus displayed anger and passion admittedly far more descriptive of a radical than a liberal. Even so, his concerns are those that many American liberals, from Abraham Lincoln to Martin Luther King, Jr., have shared, and his ethical teachings have served as a primary inspiration for liberal social programs from St. Paul's time to our own.

How can one honestly doubt Jesus's preference for the poor, downtrodden, outcast, and stranger, over the rich and privileged who reigned, then and now, both in the secular and the spiritual realm. Throughout the gospels, Jesus's ethical injunctions far more closely approximate the teachings of the social gospel preached by liberal and liberation theologians than they do the teachings of televangelists, right-wing crusaders, therapeutic feel-good positive thinkers, or New Age self-actualizers. Jesus calls into question, as did the Hebrew prophets before him, the entire structure of privilege in which the church (today erected in his name and citing his authority) participates, as do all individuals who ignore their neighbors' pain while seeking their own fortune, whether spiritual or material. Even as the words of Isaiah were recited and neglected in the temple two thousand years ago, today Jesus's teachings are often proclaimed in church by people who have no intention of putting them into practice.

Take the parable of the Good Samaritan. We have heard this parable so many times that we automatically think of Pharisees and Levites as bad, and Samaritans as good. But, in ancient Judea, when Jesus's original listeners heard it, Samaritans were anything but good. They were unclean, outcasts, untouchables. Any commerce with them was a sin against the religious laws of the time. It was the Pharisees and Levites who were respected, not the Samaritans. To hear what Jesus is saying, we must recast this story in modern terms: Think of it as the parable of the Good Homosexual.

The tale is a simple one. A homeless man lies in the gutter. A respected minister walks by, no doubt headed for some important parish meeting to discuss the yearly canvass, or on his or her way home to write a sermon on Jesus's story of the Good Samaritan. Then a well-known and popular politician passes, perhaps musing over a speech he or she is about to deliver concerning the breakdown of the economy and our need to slash social programs in order to balance the budget without taking too much more away from defense. Neither pays the homeless man in the gutter any mind. Finally, the good homosexual comes along, comforts the man, takes him to a local service center for the homeless, and gives him a little money.

"Who," Jesus asks, "was neighbor to the man?" "The good homosexual," we answer, to which he replies, "Go, thou, and do likewise."

On its surface, Jesus's parable has nothing to do with Samaritans or homosexuals; it is a gloss on the second of the two great commandments that, according to Jesus, sum up all the others: "Love thy neighbor as thyself." But given that Jesus's fellow Judeans scorned Samaritans, holding them unworthy to be treated with a full complement of neighborliness, one can deduce from this parable what Jesus might have preached from an American pulpit today concerning such social issues as homelessness and AIDS.

Today's biblical literalists would consider my reconstruction of the parable of the Good Samaritan blasphemy. They would even be able to cite a handful of scriptural injunctions condemning homosexuality to prove their case.

There is nothing new in this. The Pharisees—biblical literalists of Jesus's own day—took a similar tack: "This man Jesus is associating with Samaritans," they said. "Not only that, but he drank from the cup of a Samaritan woman, drawn from her well, which he called holy. He even touched a woman who was in the throes of her period, compounding the uncleanliness. Not to mention that he cavorted with prostitutes and other reprobates. Scripture and tradition both clearly state that Samaritans are unclean, adultery cannot be forgiven, and women must be shunned during their period. Even as this man Jesus has broken the Sabbath commandment, he continues to spurn the Torah. How can he call himself a Rabbi, and how can others call him the Messiah, when his teachings are so clearly blasphemous?"

When discussing the fine points of scripture, right-wing moralists, many of them deeply religious and sincerely devout, would find themselves more comfortable in the company of Pharisees—who were far better people than the gospels give them credit for being—than they would in the company of their savior. When discussing social programs, they would likely have felt more at home with the Sadducees. In Jesus's day, the Pharisees were conservative in theology and liberal in social philosophy; the Sadducees were lax theologically while defending the status quo, that is, the rich got richer and the poor got poorer.

I can't claim any better for myself. My chosen company would have likely been the same, only in reverse order. I'd be sharing theological prejudices with the Sadducees and plotting ethical reform with the Pharisees.

Not Jesus. He preferred prostitutes and prodigal children to both moralists and materialists. Compared to the former, society's outcasts had fewer pretensions to virtue; compared to the latter, many of them had stronger claims. He even associated with tax collectors, who were far more justifiably despised than anyone who ever audited for the IRS. In Judea taxes ran up to 80 percent of earnings, and tax collectors skimmed their own meager earnings off the top.

If Jesus's disdain toward religious authorities and the rich bespeak a radical temperament, his open and nondoctrinaire approach to the scriptures, and his preference for the spirit over the letter express a liberal religious attitude, as does his emphasis on concrete acts of service, especially to the outcast and downtrodden. Any preacher who wishes to invoke Jesus's authority on social issues, whether the question of minority rights or the tragedies of homelessness and AIDS, needs to remember two things. First, Jesus himself was not a biblical literalist; second, he had only one test for righteousness, the test of neighborliness: "Did you feed the hungry, clothe the naked, visit those in prison, heal the sick? If you were neighborly to the least of these, you were neighborly to me." Mother Teresa got it right when she said of people with AIDS, "Each of them is Jesus in distressing disguise."

I would propose that other so-called moral issues be viewed from the same liberal perspective. For a single case study, let's consider the question of prayer in the public schools. Would Jesus have been in favor of it? Manifestly not. Jesus deeply believed that, apart from corporate worship, prayer is a private act. He said that we should not pray in public, making a display of our piety, but only in private, in our own closet he said, where we could speak directly to God without distraction or presumption. Reduced to a mechanical and perfunctory act, prayer is trivialized. Prayer was so important to Jesus that he would surely have decried this. Imagine his response to twenty seconds of mechanical recitation of a prayer so watered down that it would offend almost no one.

Those with the greatest stake in this controversy are not atheists who do not believe in prayer anyway but Jews and Christians who do. Any attempt to secularize and mass market what should be a solemn encounter with God can only cheapen its meaning. Those who advocate prayer or the teaching of religious doctrine in public schools may think they are advancing the cause of Jesus. They are completely mistaken.

Beyond this, any proposal that would hitch the religious star to a state wagon reveals a profound disrespect of religion. Any religion so weak that its survival depends on the support of government is unworthy of the name. Laws ostensibly championing religion have a tendency to compromise the very thing they propose to buttress, by creating a dependency on the government, which may easily lead to a loss of moral integrity.

Devout Christian and pioneer educator Noah Webster warned us of this just over two centuries ago. Conceding that the Bible proved useful for the teaching of reading and spelling because it was the one book every family owned, Webster doubted the other claim made for it, namely that reading and teaching the scriptures in school would impress upon young minds the important truths of religion and morality. "If people design the doctrines of the Bible as a system of religion, ought they to appropriate the book to purposes foreign to this design?" Webster asked in a 1787 essay on *The Education of Youth in America*. "Will not a familiarity, contracted by a careless, disrespectful reading of the sacred volume, weaken the influence of its precepts upon the heart?"

Weighing the evidence, is not the spirit of Jesus clearly best served by the "liberal agenda" to keep the teachings of (not about) religion out of the schools? Two centuries ago, Noah Webster thought so. When he said, writing of the separation of church and state, that "The American constitutions are the most liberal in this particular of any on earth," Webster spoke as a champion of religion, not a censor. "Christianity spread with rapidity before the temporal powers interfered," he argued, "but when the civil magistrate undertook to guard the truth from error, its progress was obstructed, the simplicity of the gospel was corrupted with human inventions. . . . Every interference of the civil power in regulating opinion is an impious attempt to take the business of the Deity out of His own hands."

In all matters of church and state, the question followers of Jesus must ask when tempted by the vision either of a Christian nation or of a government actively supporting Christian teachings, is whether such a partnership advances or retards the gospel of Jesus.

One need look no farther than Western Europe today, where state religions are still established under law in several countries. Far from ensuring the strength of these institutions, state protection and financial support compromise them. No longer a free institution with independent moral authority, the church becomes a creature of the state, a pensioner. More than any other single factor, this "advantageous" arrangement, in which the established church is "honored" by preferential treatment and supported by state funds, has contributed to the decline of religion.

Three years ago, then Bishop of Stockholm Krister Stendahl preached a sharply worded sermon upbraiding certain rich Swedes for establishing their primary residence in other countries in order to avoid paying taxes in Sweden, where the tax rate runs just slightly below that of ancient Judea. Stendahl argued that this flight was a selfish and morally reprehensible act, one that deprived all their countrypeople from a higher quality of government services, from healthcare to social security benefits. Instead of rallying the less-privileged to his cause, the good bishop (and he truly is a good man) was branded a hypocrite. From the same tax base he received his salary and his church its support. In a country where the archbishop is paid more handsomely than the prime minister, Stendahl's words, though true, rang hollow, striking even those who might agree with him as potentially self-serving. Not surprisingly, this sermon caused an uproar, permitting those in the press who had long since lost interest in religion to point out that during many worship services in the cathedral the clergy outnumber the congregants.

There is one part of Europe today where religion is strong: behind what was once the Iron Curtain. If ironic, this is hardly surprising. After all, the communist governments suppressed religion for years, restricting belief, limiting worship, and monitoring religious organizations, often by means of undercover operatives. Compared to state support for religion, this was a godsend.

That doesn't mean that there was no collusion between church and state behind the Iron Curtain. In 1983, well before the thaw in the cold war, I spent ten days in Hungary as a member of a small interfaith delegation. We were sent to observe the level of freedom of conscience and religious belief. Most of the religious leaders with whom we spoke professed satisfaction with the situation. Later we learned that, in exchange for cooperating with the "minister of cults," many received supplementary stipends from the government and special dispensations on apartments. The Unitarian bishop was particularly pleased that he had just received a tiny state grant for the reprinting of a fifty-year-old biography of the founder of the Unitarian Church in Hungary, Francis David—a fillip in acknowledgment of a "cooperative" attitude.

Ironically, David, a Reformation figure, was a great prophet of freedom of religious expression. Even as the spirit of Jesus is often held captive by churches established in his name, David's name was being honored while the faith he stood for was quietly bartered away in exchange for a few dollars and an extra bedroom.

There were clergy and laypeople in every communion who refused to be co-opted, but only one group we visited, the Baptists, seemed fully independent of the state. They suffered for it, but their faith didn't. Like the Catholics in Poland, evangelicals in the Soviet Union, and some Lutherans in East Germany, co-option grew stronger in direct proportion to the level of government opposition and interference.

Still, the best religious argument in favor of the separation of church and state is manifest in the vitality of religion in the United States today. By almost every measure, religion is far stronger here than in those European countries where the church receives state support, as well as in most of those where it has been repressed. On a regular basis, 40 percent of Americans frequent church or synagogue compared to fewer than 5 percent in England, Sweden, West Germany, or France. If nothing else, enlightened self-interest should persuade religious advocates of prayer in the public schools and other public support for religious institutions that such support is counterproductive.

We are slow in learning this lesson. As far back as the original debate over the First Amendment, which draws a clear line separating church and state, Representative Peter Sylvester of New York claimed that such a law "might be thought to have a tendency to abolish religion altogether." In response, Baptist Minister John Leland dismissed the "religious" argument in favor of state support with these words:

> What stimulates the clergy to recommend this mode of reasoning is, (1) Ignorance—not being able to confute error by fair argument. (2) Indolence—not being willing to spend any time to confute the heretical. (3) But chiefly covetousness, to get money—for it may be observed that in all these establishments settled salaries for the clergy recoverable by law are sure to be interwoven.

Even earlier, near the turn of the eighteenth century, Colonel Lewis Morris, an Anglican laymen from New York, had argued that his church would be far better off without state support, including state funds to underwrite clergy salaries. In his view, the church would have been "in much better condition had there been no Act in her favor; for in the Jersies and Pennsylvania where there is not Act in her favor, there is four times the number of Churchmen than there is in this province of New York, and they are so most of them upon principle."

He was right. Religion prospers in the United States today, uncompromised by the taint of government collusion, because of the wall between church and state. The authors of our Bill of Rights understood this, as have enlightened political and religious leaders from our founding as a nation until the present day.

Included in their number are many evangelicals, who, convinced that the realm of the spirit lies beyond the purview of government, vigorously support maintenance of the constitutional proscription of laws relating to religion. Throughout our history, the liberal spirit that informed our nation's founders is complemented and buttressed by the "evangelical separatism" of those who recognize the profound importance of preserving complete religious liberty.

Historically, few religious bodies have witnessed more eloquently the principles of religious freedom and church–state separation than the Baptists. In our country, Roger Williams, a Baptist preacher, was the greatest early prophet of religious toleration and liberty. Rhode Island, the state he founded, became the model for our national policy of strict separation between matters of state and matters of religion. Yet, even as Francis David's tradition was betrayed by latter-day Unitarians in Hungary, Roger Williams's tradition has received a like sentence in some Southern Baptist circles. They have forgotten what Williams knew so well: Whether the state is dictating to the church, as was the case behind the Iron Curtain, or the church is dictating to the state, as some Christians in the United States continue to urge, the entity most certain to be compromised and to suffer is not the state but the church.

Baptists in Hungary recognized this truth. So did Baptists in seventeenth-century America, and Episcopalians such as George Washington a century later. So did Saint Paul, who said, "Where the Spirit of the Lord is, there is Liberty" (2 Cor. 3:10). This is the spirit by which our religious and political forebears were guided: the spirit of tolerance and freedom, the spirit of Jesus, the liberal spirit.

This is certainly true of Thomas Jefferson, who went so far as to extract from the gospels all those sayings of Jesus that he considered to be genuine, compiling them for his own devotional purposes in a little book entitled *The Life and Morals of Jesus of Nazareth*. Sorting out "passages of fine imagination, correct morality, and of the most lovely benevolence," and placing these teachings in four columns (Greek, Latin, English, and French), Jefferson declared that the fragments remaining comprise a "system of morality [that] was the most benevolent and sublime probably that has been ever taught, and consequently more perfect than those of any of the ancient philosophers."

In 1820, Jefferson described his compilation in a letter to a Unitarian friend, William Short:

> We find in the writings of [Jesus's] biographers matter of two distinct descriptions. First, a groundwork of vulgar ignorance, of things impossible, of superstitions, fanaticisms and fabrications. Intermixed with these, again, are sublime ideas of the Supreme Being, aphorisms, and precepts of the purest morality and benevolence, sanctioned by a life of humility, innocence, and simplicity of manners, neglect of riches, absence of worldly ambition and honors, with an eloquence and persuasiveness that have not been surpassed.

The process of highlighting or selecting certain passages in the scriptures as a guide for one's own personal reflections is not as heretical as it may seem. Martin Luther had no use for the book of Revelation, and described the letter of James as "the straw epistle." All preachers and theologians have their favorite texts, which color and shape their theology, and inform their understanding of Jesus's nature and teachings. Beyond this, since the mid-nineteenth century many biblical scholars have done precisely what Jefferson himself did somewhat earlier: attempt to discriminate between those teachings most likely to have been spoken by Jesus and others added later by his biographers.

Thomas Jefferson's search was not so much for the historical as for the intelligible Jesus, an ethical teacher whose insights span the centuries with continuing impact and relevance. John Adams recognized as much when he wrote, "I admire your employment in selecting the philosophy and divinity of Jesus, and separating it from all mixtures. If I had eyes and nerves I would go through both Testaments and mark all that I understand." Neither man was a theologian, but both were sincere students of religion, and each was guided by the light of a liberal Jesus, whose teachings complemented and undergirded their own vision of a just, merciful, and equitable society.

Invoking the same liberal spirit, the spirit of neighborliness,

President George Washington closed his eloquent farewell address with these words:

> I now make it my earnest prayer that God would have you . . . entertain a brotherly affection and love for one another, . . . that He would most graciously be pleased to dispose us all to do justice, to love mercy, and to demean ourselves with that charity, humility, and pacific temper of mind which were the characteristics of the Divine Author of our blessed religion, and without a humble imitation of whose example in these things we can never hope to be a happy nation.

Whether Jesus was the second greatest liberal of all time remains arguable. But if he was not, our nation's founders were just as mistaken as I.

# 3

# *The Holy Spirit*

Where the Spirit of the Lord is there is Liberty.
—St. Paul (1 Cor. 3:18)

In traditional Christian theology, God is represented as a trinity—three persons in one substance—Father, Son, and Holy Spirit. For many, including theologians, the third person in this trinity is the most difficult to conceptualize. Perhaps that is because, unlike the Father, who is often understood as wholly transcendent, and the Son, conceived by many as God's presence uniquely incarnate in a man who lived nearly two thousand years ago, the Holy Spirit is presented, even by orthodox Christian teachers, as the Spirit of God within and among us, unimaginably close at hand. The great neo-orthodox theologian, Karl Barth, defined "God's Spirit, the Holy Spirit," as God, so far as God "cannot only come to human beings, but be in them."

Like many of our country's founders, including Thomas Jefferson and John Adams, I am a Unitarian. By strict definition, a Unitarian is one who believes that God is not a trinity but a unity. This conviction grew initially out of a searching review of the scriptures, where evidence for the existence of a triune God is at best only sporadically implicit, and never actually proclaimed. The trinitarian doctrine was not codified until the Council of Nicea, nearly three centuries after the death of Jesus. From that date forward, it became the prism through which the light of the scriptural evidence concerning God was refracted into three parts and thus interpreted.

Today, what distinguishes Unitarianism from many other denominations is not so much its rejection of the trinity but rather its nondoctrinal nature, and the emphasis it places on freedom of religious belief. Trusting the evidence of deeds, not creeds, as proof of our religious integrity, and recognizing the limits of our knowledge, each Unitarian Universalist (the two liberal denominations merged in 1961) is free to interpret the mystery of God according to his or her own experience and understanding.

Given this liberty, I am one Unitarian Universalist who finds the trinitarian prism helpful. Rather than a single, undifferentiated light, the nuances of trinitarianism (God the creator; God the savior; God the living presence, comforter, and prophetic spirit) offer, for me at least, a more poetic and suggestive opportunity for contemplating the mystery of God. Yet, of the three bands of the trinitarian spectrum, I still find one especially illuminating. To the extent that I am a unitarian, doctrinally as well as denominationally, I am a unitarian not of God the Father, as were Jefferson and Adams, but of God the Holy Spirit.

Throughout the Bible, the Holy Spirit is nothing less than a liberal *agent provocateur,* with liberty its watchword. Like the wind, it "bloweth where it listeth, and thou hearest the sound thereof, but canst not tell whence it cometh, and whither it goeth: so is every one that is born of the Spirit" (John 3:8).

The words for spirit in the scriptures are *ruah* in the Hebrew, and *pneuma* (a feminine noun) in the Greek. Each has its own particular set of nuances, but both share two basic meanings, "wind" and "breath." The Latin parallel, *spiritus*, is the root for our words expire (to breathe out for the last time), inspired (to be filled with the spirit), and aspire (to reach toward).

It is easy to see how this word became endowed with divine characteristics. Both wind and breath blow freely and mysteriously. They are invisible, yet powerful: We see and feel only their effect. We receive the breath of life. The winds waft from heaven. When we blow on a flute, our breath is turned to music. In like measure, it is taught that when the spirit of God fills us, we become God's instruments. Since the spirit is both beyond us and within us, theologians soon perceived this modality of God as the most intimate link of communication between the material and the spiritual worlds, the natural and the divine, ourselves and God.

Defining the Holy Spirit as God within and among us, the spirit's presence becomes most clearly manifest in Godly words and deeds. The two cannot be divorced, for without deeds even the most eloquent and impassioned words are empty. In the Bible, this theme recurs throughout the writings of the prophets, where the spirit of God is most often directly invoked. More specifically, the presence of the spirit is almost always coupled with a stirring cry for justice, or liberty with equity.

This is especially clear in the Book of Isaiah. The prophet first announces that God's servant, who was heretofore himself a slave, is to be anointed with the Holy Spirit: "The Spirit of the Lord shall alight upon him. . . . He shall judge the poor with equity and decide with justice for the lowly of the land" (Isaiah 11:1ff). Later, according to prophetic prerogative, Isaiah speaks for God directly, saying, "I have put my spirit upon him. . . . He shall not break even a bruised reed, or snuff out even a dim wick. He shall bring forth the true way" (Isaiah 42:1, 3). Finally, the servant himself speaks: "The Spirit of the Lord God is upon me. . . . He hath sent me to bind up the brokenhearted, to proclaim liberty to the captives, and the opening of the prison to them that are bound" (Isaiah 61:1).

This vision, offered by prophets inspired by the spirit, is clearly utopian. Its goal is to approximate the Realm of God on earth. Admittedly, utopians can become fanatical, blindly convinced that they alone are righteous. Possessed of holy ends, they may resort to unholy means to establish an earthly paradise. The Christian Crusades were waged to liberate Jerusalem and thus prepare for the coming of the Kingdom. The dictatorship of the proletariat promised a just and equitable society. In each case, hubris invited nemesis, and at an enormous cost. In this century alone, millions of innocents have perished on the altar of utopian ideology.

Today, radical liberation theologians sometimes succumb to the same danger. Compromising their clarity of vision with regard to atrocities on the right, a blind eye is turned to those on the left. Decades of oppression in Eastern Europe have passed almost completely unnoticed by liberation theologians entranced by the allure of Marxism. But, nonetheless, to abandon an ideal simply because we can never realize it fully, or because we may betray it in our attempts to do so, is to sacrifice the true American dream, best summed up as liberty and justice for all.

One blueprint for that dream is alluded to in the third passage from Isaiah cited above, where the Holy Spirit comes down and proclaims liberty for even the most despised members of society. Isaiah is calling for the establishment of "the acceptable year of the Lord," a year in which slaves would be liberated, the prisons emptied, and the poor given land of their own. In the Book of Leviticus, this is referred to as the Jubilee, which falls, after seven times seven years, on the fiftieth year, as a great Sabbath of reconciliation. In our own nation's history, the song of the Jubilee sounded forth in 1865, in a stirring chorus of newly liberated slaves:

> Every nigger's gwine to own a mule,
>   Jubili, Jubilo!
> Every nigger's gwine to own a mule,
> An' live like Adam in de Golden Rule,
> An' send his chillun to de white folks' school!
>   In de year of Jubilo!

However fitting to the occasion, this is not the first time that the promised Jubilee sounded in our history. Coupling the dream of the prophets with the vision of our nation's founders, it is also given voice on the Liberty Bell, engraved there in a motto taken directly from Leviticus.

On July 4, 1957, my father, Frank Church, delivered the annual Fourth of July address at Independence Hall in Philadelphia. It was his first major address since his election eight months before as United States senator from Idaho. Playing a few changes on the traditional Independence Day theme, he devoted his remarks to the relationship between liberty and peace. He called upon America to renew its devotion to liberty by "waging peace with the same zeal and determination with which we have waged war." He invoked—as did the founding fathers in the Declaration of Independence—"the Supreme Judge of the world for the rectitude of our intentions," while warning that "Our liberty itself is in danger of being stifled in the very cause of defending it."

I don't remember being there to hear him speak these words, but someone took a picture that hangs in my study—my parents, maternal grandparents, and I standing in front of the Liberty Bell, touching it for good luck. My father was thirty-two years old; I was eight.

"Patriotism is love of country," my father continued. "How does one love his country?" he asked. "One loves his country as one loves his own child—with a will to serve its inmost needs and to see it reach fulfillment; to dream its best dreams, to labor to make them come true." In the course of a brief address, he linked love of God, love of country, and love of family, each of which requires us to honor, nurture, and enhance the spirit of liberty.

Commissioned for the Pennsylvania statehouse in 1751 to mark the Golden Jubilee of William Penn's "Charter of Privileges," the Liberty Bell has played a significant supporting role in our history. Though it did not, as legend has it, toll to commemorate the signing of the Declaration of Independence, it did stand sentinel as the Second Continental Congress performed its momentous work in 1776, and also again eleven years later on September 17, 1787, when Congress met in Philadelphia to adopt the Federal Constitution.

Before it rang true, the Liberty Bell had to be cast three times: once to no one's satisfaction by a foundry in England;

and twice more, first poorly and then well, in America. One thing that continued unchanged throughout the castings was the motto engraved on it: "Proclaim liberty throughout all the land unto all the inhabitants thereof."

These words are taken from the proclamation of Jubilee in Leviticus 25, which spells out the covenant between Yahweh and his people. "The Lord said to Moses on Mount Sinai, 'Say to the people of Israel, When you come into the land which I give you, the land shall keep a sabbath to the Lord,' " during which all, including slaves, servants, and sojourners, shall be freely fed and cared for. Every fifty years, after seven such cycles, a great sabbath will take place, the year of Jubilee, during which all debts will be forgiven; slaves freed together with their families; land and shelter, fields and homes, released and distributed to those who otherwise could not afford them. "If your brother becomes poor, and cannot maintain himself with you, you shall maintain him; as a stranger and a sojourner he shall live with you. Take not interest from him or increase, but fear your God; that your brother may live beside you . . . over your brethren the people of Israel you shall not rule, one over another, with harshness."

The Jubilee year, that year acceptable to the Lord, offers one vision, a decidedly liberal vision, of what the Realm of God might be like were it ever to be established. Described as the sabbath of sabbaths, according to many ancient interpreters it corresponds directly with the seventh day of creation. This is not only the day when God is said to have rested (having deemed that all was good) but also the day of the new creation, when the world (which turned out to be far from perfect) would be redeemed, the day when all might share and share alike the bounties of liberty. "Behold," Isaiah prophesies, giving voice to God's new plan, "I create new heavens and a new earth; and the former things shall not be remembered or come into mind" (Isaiah 65:17).

As best described by the prophet Joel, when this new world is established the Holy Spirit will be poured out liberally over all, creating a true democracy in which young and old, rich and poor, slave and free, male and female will share equally in the divine blessing:

> I will pour out My spirit on all flesh;
> Your sons and daughters shall prophesy;
> Your old men shall dream dreams.
> And your young men shall see visions.
> I will even pour out My spirit
> Upon male and female slaves in those days. (Joel 3)

This dream-vision is clearly utopian, but it does have practical applications, especially when one considers the broader implications of the sabbath commandment.

Placed in the context of the Jubilee year—and the new creation on the seventh day—what does the Holy Spirit require of us on our own sabbaths? Is it enforcement of Blue Laws or of the Golden Rule? Clearly the latter. By establishing a day of rest, which precludes all authorities, parents to land barons, from enforcing labor upon their children, servants, guests, and even their animals, the sabbath commandment dashes all temporal distinctions and thus offers a glimpse into the true nature of God's Commonwealth: both a spiritual and material democracy. On the Lord's day, all are equal—husbands and wives, parents and children, employers and employees, strikingly even humans and animals. Since no one serves another, all are free to serve God.

This touches the heart of the liberal social gospel, summed up by Jesus as love to God and love to neighbor. In this case the two are the same.

The question remains, since we cannot hope to realize the holy vision of liberty with equity for all, to what extent can we approximate it in our covenants with one another. Since the spirit moves in mysterious ways, one answer comes from an unexpected source, Oliver Cromwell. In 1647, he was threatened from without by Parliament and from within by division between his own group, the Independents (mostly officers) who supported only limited democracy, and his opponents, the Levellers (mostly soldiers) who demanded universal suffrage. The Presbyterian general urged both sides to seek the guidance of the Holy Spirit. Already he had expanded his council to include greater representation from the regiments, in order that "there may be a liberal and free debate had amongst us, that we may understand really, as before God, the bottom of our desires, and that we may seek God together, and see if God will give us an uniting spirit." Now he called on them "to see what God will direct you to say to us, that whilst we are going one way, and you another, we be not both destroyed."

How could they know that the Holy Spirit indeed was present in their midst, working with them in their deliberations? How can any of us know if our chosen path is inspired by the Holy Spirit? "I do not know any outward evidence of what proceeds from the Spirit of God more clear than this," Cromwell told both parties: "the appearance of meekness and gentleness and mercy and patience and forbearance and love, and a desire to do good to all and to destroy none that can be saved." Cromwell himself was not always able to live up to his own words, but with biblical cadence and simplicity they offer as good a test as any I know for determining whether the Holy Spirit is present or excluded from our own councils and communities.

Such testing is important, for the word *spirit* also has a negative connotation. In both Hebrew and Greek, not only does it signify the breath of life and the wind from heaven, inspiring us to works of love and deeds of praise. It also represents other vapors, rising from the bowels of the earth, an unhealthy spirit that could possess or seduce us, releasing demonic, sometimes fatal powers. Plato warned that the spirit could fill people with power, yet rob them of understanding. He was describing mantic behavior, not unlike what in Christian circles, both in New Testament times and today, could be called speaking in tongues. From the earliest times, both prophetic and ecstatic utterance were considered inspired, but because of the ambiguity between divine and diabolical inspiration, some further test was required to differentiate between the two.

According to the biblical story of Elijah and the prophets of Baal, for every true prophet there are likely to be 450 false ones. We must therefore be mindful of the biblical warning to discriminate between spirits. Rasputin was inspired; so was Hitler. Hitler was inspired, ironically enough, by a vision of purity. He was a teetotaler and a vegetarian. His own obsession with purity had demonic consequences in the genocide of the Jews who did not fit his dream of a hermetically sealed pure and Aryan nation. The words *spirit* and *conspirator* stem from the same root. Conspirators are people who breathe the same air, often the rank air of religious bigotry, or sexism, or racism, or any kind of chauvinism that divides us one from another.

In attempting to discriminate between spirits, the adjective *holy* is helpful. It goes back to the Teutonic root meaning, whole, from which we also get the words *hale* and *healthy.* Its parallel in Latin is *salve*. People in ancient Rome would wish one another *salve* or *salvate*—"Be well." We say farewell, which is related to adieu or good-bye, each of which means "God be with you." The relationship is evident in another word that springs from the same root: That word is salvation.

If salvation means wholeness, haleness, and holiness, the holy spirit, as an instrument of salvation, is that which unites us with our better selves, demands reconciliation with our neighbor, and inspires oneness with God. For the Hebrews and many early Christians, the test for this was simple: By their fruits you shall know them. Since the Holy Spirit is the spirit of liberty, its fruits must be liberation, justice, and equity. Or, in Paul's words, "The fruit of the spirit is love, joy, peace, longsuffering, gentleness, goodness, and faith" (Galatians 5:22). This means only those whose prophesy facilitates the creation of redemptive community may be said to be inspired by God. When it comes to judging between one charismatic leader and another—between people who inspire passionate followings—we can best sort good from evil, the divine from the diabolic, by imposing the test of wholeness, or holiness.

The question is, Do they use their power to bring us together, or to divide us against one another?

This may have little to do with personal morality. The personal morality of Adolf Hitler was beyond reproach. He was a paragon of temperance and moderation. None of this can be said about Martin Luther King, Jr. When we move from individual morals to the larger question of societal ethics, the test of holiness has little to do with moralism. Few people of our century have been more clearly inspired by the Holy Spirit than Martin Luther King, Jr. Not only did he fight for his own people but he fought for all of us by refusing to fight with violence. He relied on the sacred authority of his cause, grounded both in scripture and the visionary blueprints of our republic.

Such distinctions are important, because those possessed with or by the chrism of the spirit do have greater power, both for good and for evil, than others do. We must always weigh their words in the balance of their public deeds. Otherwise we run the danger of being enthralled by personal magnetism, rather than swept up in the goodness of a shared cause. Charismatic political leaders and evangelists may be false prophets who build small empires—not for God or their country but for themselves—by playing on people's neediness, credulity, and especially their prejudices and fears. Though personal sins, such as adultery, may cause them to fall, these are mere peccadillos compared to the blasphemy that some of them commit against the Holy Spirit.

Even the ancient prophets did not speak as individuals, when speaking in the spirit. They spoke for the people, the whole community. And their witness was confirmed precisely to the extent that all members of that community—rich and poor, male and female, slave and free—were fully included in the divine dispensation. Anyone who invokes the scriptures to enforce divisiveness, bigotry, and neighborly hate is guilty of blasphemy against the Holy Spirit, the only sin that Jesus said could not be forgiven.

There is a tendency, not unique to twentieth-century Americans but exaggerated by our own penchant for individualism, to privatize the spirit. I think of many so-called New Age afficionados, who devote their spiritual energy to getting in touch with past lives, tapping the power of crystals, or even feeling their bliss. Much New Age teaching has universal spiritual relevance, reminding us that there are powers beyond our own that we often neglect. And few of that increasing number of people whose religious quest leads them from one workshop to another do any real harm. If they feel better about themselves and their lives, they may even do some small good, be kinder to their neighbors, a little easier to live with.

But none of this has anything to do with building a just and equitable society. Like the mystery cults during Jesus's day, there are New Age religions that are self-serving and elitist (only those with $250 for a weekend need apply). Representing a kind of disembodied spiritualism, with each seeker on a private quest for esoteric knowledge and personal salvation, this form of religion is basically self-help religion. Rather than leading to the love of God and our neighbor as ourself, it posits the following heretical tautology: the love of God and ourself as God.

The Christian church continued, while the mystery cults and gnostic conventicles failed, because Jesus followed in the spirit of the prophets. Love took precedence over knowledge, and the good of the community, both spiritual and material, could not be distinguished from the good of the individual. As Paul said, "In Christ there is neither male nor female, neither slave nor free." Most mystery cults limited their membership to men with property. The early Christian churches included both women and slaves as full members of their fellowship, and devoted their offerings to widows and orphans. Fashioning their communities according to the Holy Spirit, they aspired to model a commonwealth of love, its emblem liberty to all, to be guaranteed by equitable treatment of each, regardless of status or station.

The church could not sustain this vision. Religious institutions, with all their worldly baggage, rarely do. Early on there were divisions within the Christian community. But most often those divisions were caused not by Christians who were insufficiently devout but by men and women who claimed spiritual superiority over their brothers and sisters by boasting of some special knowledge or gift.

St. Paul confronted this in the church at Corinth. Like certain of today's Pentecostals, some early Christians, among them many in Corinth, thought that the most important evidence of possession by the Holy Spirit was glossalalia, or speaking in tongues. None could make sense of their inspired utterance, but those who demonstrated this gift became a spiritual elite, considered both by themselves and many others more holy and privileged than their brothers and sisters.

Paul did not discount speaking in tongues as a gift, but he did believe, with Jesus and the prophets, that the Holy Spirit comes to unite rather than divide us, and that true religious community, anticipating the Realm of God, honors all members alike. He beseeched the Christians in Corinth to remember that "There are varieties of gifts, but the same Spirit; and there are varieties of service, but the same Lord; and there are varieties of working, but it is the same God who inspires them all in every one. To each is given the manifestation of the Spirit for the common good." Then, in the spirit of Isaiah and Joel, Paul offered another metaphor for redemptive community, one that pertains as much to the liberal body politic as to the body of Christ.

> Just as the body is one and has many members, and all the members of the body, though many, are one body, so it is with Christ. For by one Spirit were we all baptized into one body—Jews or Greeks, slaves or free—and all were made to drink of one Spirit. . . . If all were a single organ, where would the body be? As it is, there are many parts, yet one body. The eye cannot say to the hand, "I have no need of you," nor again the head to the feet, "I have no need of you." On the contrary, the parts of the body which seem to be weaker are indispensable, and those

> parts of the body which we think less honorable we invest with the greatest honor. . . . God has so composed the body, giving the greater honor to the inferior part, that there may be no discord in the body, but that the members may have the same care for one another. If one member suffers, all suffer together; if one member is honored, all rejoice together. (1 Cor. 12)

Though Paul is speaking only of the Christian community, today a growing number of theologians confront the reality of religious pluralism by proposing the Holy Spirit as that modality of God present to all, without regard to faith.

This is certainly the spirit in which Isaiah and Joel spoke. It is the spirit of universalism, offering mercy to all, embracing a vision for community based on reconciliation, not division—the very ideal upon which our own liberal democracy is founded. To approximate it we must honor the least among us as we do the greatest. According to Isaiah and implicit in the words of Paul, we must even go so far as to show preferential treatment for the poor, the outcast, indeed for all those whom society has slighted or forgotten.

Another depiction of true spiritual community surfaces in the New Testament. It is the story of Pentecost as recounted by Luke in the Book of Acts. Fifty days (a Jubilee interval) after his death, the disciples of Jesus gathered, "and suddenly a sound came from heaven like the rush of a mighty wind, and it filled all the house where they were sitting. . . . And they were all filled with the Holy Spirit and began to speak in other tongues, as the Spirit gave them utterance." Unlike those in Corinth who prided themselves for speaking in tongues that no one could understand, when these people spoke in tongues, people from every nation under heaven came to listen, "and they were bewildered because each one heard them speaking in his own language" (Acts 2:2–5). Once again, the Holy Spirit is the spirit of unity, not division. People come together, retain their individuality, are protected in their diversity, and yet, at the same time, are one.



CAMAS PUBLIC LIBRARY

When the Pennsylvania legislators chose to engrave on our Liberty Bell these words from Leviticus—"Proclaim liberty throughout the land to all the inhabitants thereof"—they pledged themselves to as liberal and expansive a mission as any people can undertake, the establishment of a society based on liberty for all. They were surely not unmindful of the biblical context from which this declaration is taken: the proclamation of "the acceptable year of the Lord"; a year not of wrath but of reconciliation; a year of jubilation, with all of God's children given equal cause to celebrate; the promised seventh day, of rest and new creation; the year of Jubilee.

They failed to live up to this dream. We shall fail as well. If the Commonwealth of God on earth should ever come—that realm in which all shall receive alike the blessings of freedom and justice as proclaimed in the Bible by prophets inspired by the Holy Spirit—it will be in God's good time. But we are accountable for one thing. We are accountable every time we betray the spirit of this liberal vision, either by word or by deed.

In 1777, with the British marching on Philadelphia, the Continental Congress recommended, and the Supreme Executive Council agreed and ordered, all bells to be removed and hidden, lest they be stolen and melted down for bullets. A group of patriots took the Liberty Bell to Allentown, Pennsylvania, where it was stored in the basement of the Zion Reformed Church. Once the danger had passed, they returned it to the State House, where it pealed out the surrender of General Cornwallis in Yorktown in 1781. Fifty-four years later, while being rung during the funeral of the great jurist, Chief Justice John Marshall, the Liberty Bell cracked.

This too is a symbol, at least a reminder that the spirit of liberty is fragile. That the bell itself cracked means little. But if the spirit expressed by its motto—the spirit of the prophets, the liberal spirit of our founders—is forgotten, then the dream it represents will begin to die: justice to the poor, to women, to minorities; the rights of conscience; religious liberty; freedom of speech.

Fortunately, we have many reminders. In New York Harbor the Statue of Liberty greets stranger and sojourner alike, shining a beacon of hope, proclaiming liberty to all, especially the least among us. As Catholic theologian and social critic Michael Novak points out, she is "the highest liberal symbol in New York City." A woman, not a warrior, she holds a torch of freedom in one hand, and a book, not a gun, in the other. What she represents is no different really than that vision of the prophets.

In 1883, the Jewish poet Emma Lazarus was asked by the chairman of the committee raising funds to build a pedestal for the statue to contribute a sonnet that might highlight its significance. She called it "The New Colossus," so markedly different in every way from the ancient Colossus of Rhodes.

> Not like the brazen giant of Greek fame,
> With conquering limbs astride from land to land;
> Here at our sea-washed, sunset gates shall stand
> A mighty woman with a torch, whose flame
> Is the imprisoned lightning, and her name
> Mother of Exiles. From her beacon-hand
> Glows world-wide welcome; her mild eyes command
> The air-bridged harbor that twin cities frame.

And then those famous lines. Could not Isaiah himself have said, when prompted by the Holy Spirit:

> Give me your tired, your poor,
> Your huddled masses yearning to breathe free,
> The wretched refuse of your teeming shore,
> Send these, the homeless, tempest-tost to me:
> I lift my lamp beside the golden door.

No wonder that the Chinese students in Tiananmen Square, just shortly before they were routed and so many of them were massacred by government soldiers on June 10, 1989, erected their own replica of the Statue of Liberty, a 32-foot-high "freedom goddess," and placed it in the center of the square. And no wonder that the songs they sang that day were religious hymns, spirituals, and anthems: "A Mighty Fortress is Our God"; "We Shall Overcome"; and "Bridge Over Troubled Waters."

They didn't just hum along, as we sometimes do. Whether with their voices or their spirits, they sang together in a single chorus, and knew exactly what the words meant, and how much they meant—even those among them who didn't know a word of our language.

It shouldn't be surprising. As Isaiah, Paul, or Abraham Lincoln could have told us, that is how the Holy Spirit works.

# II

# *Reclaiming the Flag*

# 4

# *With Liberty for All*

They would use their own liberty, for none had power to command them.

—William Bradford, *History of Plymouth Plantation*

Far from being established only when we declared independence in 1776, liberty was both sought and employed by our Puritan forebears when they settled in America during the early seventeenth century. Not that they always lived up to the premise of the scriptures in which they placed their faith. Having established liberty for themselves, they were chary of extending it to those with whom they disagreed. Even so, several major themes that play throughout our nation's history are first struck by the early European settlers, whose goals were as noble as the scriptures upon which they were founded.

When John Winthrop and his party of Puritans on the ship *Arabella* dropped anchor off the New England coast in 1630, he took to the deck and preached a sermon containing his vision of a holy commonwealth in America. "We must consider that we shall be as a city upon a hill; the eyes of all people are upon us." He then expressed his dream for America—the first American dream: "We must delight in each other, make other's conditions our own, rejoice together, mourne together, labor and suffer together, always having before our eyes our community as members of the same body." The word he used to describe this dream was covenant.

> It is of the nature and essence of every society to be knit together by some covenant, either expressed or implied. . . . For the work we have in hand, it is by mutual consent, through a special over-ruling providence and a more than ordinary approbation of the churches of Christ, to seek out a place of cohabitation and consortship, under a due form of government both civil and ecclesiastical. . . . Therefore we must not content ourselves with usual ordinary means. Whatsoever we did or ought to have done when we lived in England, the same must we do, and more also where we go. . . . Thus stands the cause between God and us: we are entered into covenant with Him for this work; we have taken out a commission, the Lord hath given us leave to draw our own articles.

Three aspirations are implicit in these words: (1) for a community in which the rights of all would be respected; (2) for a society whose standards and achievements would be extraordinary; and (3) for a government founded on a covenant with God that granted to those who would establish liberty the freedom to do so according to their own light.

A similar spirit infused the founders of the Plymouth colony ten years before. In the Mayflower Compact, signed on November 11, 1620, after a stormy crossing of the Atlantic, the first Pilgrims covenanted and combined themselves "together into a civil body politick, for our better ordering and preservation." If the seeds of liberty were planted first in rocky New England soil, soon they would take root throughout the colonies. Not everyone came to the new world for religious reasons. Among our early settlers were aristocrats as well as vagabonds, but the Puritans far outstripped both, in influence as well as number. By conservative estimate, as late as 1776, when we declared independence from Great Britain, two-thirds of the colonists had sprung from Puritan stock.

To identify the wellspring of the Puritan spirit, one need only open the Old Testament and turn to the prophets, especially Amos, in whose prophetic demands, as church historian Sydney Ahlstrom writes, "one senses a fundamental aspect of [the Puritan] temper." In the eighth century B.C., Amos of Tekoa gazed into the heavens and perceived the work of the creator in the Pleiades and Orion. His was a God of nature who ordered the universe, at the same time establishing an ethical order on earth. For Amos, as with other prophets inspired by the Holy Spirit, evil (or ungodly behavior) manifests itself in lack of concern for the poor, a love of luxury, unfair business practices, and a general refusal to shape one's life according to God's will.

> Therefore because you trample upon the poor
> and take from him exactions of wheat,
> you have built houses of hewn stone,
> but you shall not dwell in them;
> you have planted pleasant vineyards,
> but you shall not drink their wine.
> For I know how many are your transgressions,
> and how great are your sins—
> you who afflict the righteous, who take a bribe,
> and turn aside the needy in the gate.
> Therefore he who is prudent will keep silent in such a time;
> for it is an evil time.
> Seek good, and not evil,
> that you may live;
> and so that the Lord, the God of hosts,
> will be with you,
> as you have said.
> Hate evil, and love good,
> and establish justice in the gate;
> it may be that the Lord, the God of hosts,
> will be gracious to the remnant of Joseph. (Amos 5:11–15)

As did Abraham Lincoln on one noted occasion, the Puritans asked themselves not whether God was on their side but whether they were on the side of God, for God would only be on their side if they chose to live by God's commandments. These commandments were straightforward and practical, sanctioning only needs, not extraneous wants, and requiring the establishment of a strict but fair government to enforce them. Though they did believe that honest labor, hard work, and charitable living would lead to God's blessing and earthly success, in its pure form this approach remains implicitly egalitarian. To be among the chosen was to be humbled as well as blessed. The Puritan who saw a man strung from the gallows and said "There, but for the grace of God, go I" did not elevate himself above others. He knew that in God's eye distinctions of rank and status hold no importance. This led to a revulsion against any kind of conspicuous display.

Thus the budding democratic spirit of America was well, if unintentionally, served. As historian Kenneth Minogue writes, "The aristocratic way of life, involving the development of a fashionable style of luxurious living, the wasteful consumption of food and services, is impossible to defend in these terms. Aristocratic life seemed from this point of view to be merely the wilful indulgence of desires." One recalls the old Leveller couplet, "When Adam delved and Eve span, who was then the gentleman?"

To be sure, the Massachusetts Bay Colony was a religious commonwealth, not a pluralistic democracy. This was especially true with respect to freedom of religion. As President Taft said of the Puritans in 1905, at a commemoration ceremony celebrating the anniversary of the founding of Norwich, Connecticut, "They came to this country to establish freedom of their religion, and not the freedom of anybody else's religion." Taft, a Unitarian, had an especially sharp eye for all abridgments of religious freedom, as did his co-religionist, the great nineteenth-century American historian George Bancroft, who wrote in his *History of the United States* that "Positive enactments against irreligion, like positive enactments against fanaticism, provoke the evil which they were designed to prevent." And it is true, by tying their experiments in self-governance explicitly to biblical models, the early Puritans sought a religious litmus test in order to guarantee the integrity of their governance. As late as 1701, the Rev. Samuel Torrey described the aspirations of his Puritan forebears in grandiose terms:

> When the Lord our God planted these Heavens, and laid the foundations of this Earth, and said to New England, Thou art my People: I mean when he first founded and Erected, both an Ecclesiastical and Civil Constitution here . . . and thereby made us not only a People, but His People; he put it into hearts of his Servants in both Orders to endeavour a Coalition of both those fundamental Interests, (viz.) that of Heaven, and that of Earth; which is to say, that of Religion, and that of Civil Government, that the latter might be sanctified by the former, and our Churches and People be confirmed and flourish.

Others drew an analogy between the establishment of New England and the exodus of God's people from Egypt to Israel, the promised land of milk and honey. Both peoples sought their freedom to worship as they wished. Both entered the wilderness to escape oppression. And both suffered, due not only to the exigencies of their situation but also, at least according to their preachers, for having failed to live up to the strictures imposed on them by God.

Despite these evidences of spiritual elitism, suggesting that the settlers of New England were God's new chosen people, the Puritan spirit presaged and prepared the way for liberal democracy, both through its theology and its polity. Sociologist Robert Bellah describes the embryonic emergence of liberalism in the seventeenth century, with its twin principles of progress and democracy, as "secular translations of the Protestant inner-worldly asceticism and priesthood of all believers."

There was nothing liberal about the theological narrowness and intolerance manifested by many Puritans, but two aspects of their teachings did eventually become cornerstones of the liberal democratic tradition: (1) congregational polity, which downplayed the importance of the clergy, and expressed itself in the priesthood and prophethood of all believers; and (2) the notion of individual liberty before God, giving the conscience priority over any external authority, thus enhancing both human responsibility and human dignity.

Wary of disorder and suspicious of human nature, the Puritan leaders showed little gift for democracy. John Winthrop went so far as to defend his tightly held minority rule by arguing that there was no democracy in ancient Israel. Yet, even Winthrop set up justice and mercy as the two fundamental principles that should instruct our behavior, both personal and civic. In his sermon on the *Arabella*, he took special notice of Matthew 5:54 ("If thine enemy hunger, feed him; love your enemies; do good to them that hate you"), noting that "To apply this to the works of mercy, this law requires two things: first, that every man afford his help to another in every want or distress; second, that he perform this out of the same affection which makes him careful of his own good." Biblical ideals are hard to approximate in civil settings, yet these sentiments underpin early American ideals, and continue to find expression in all the great liberal documents of our history.

An early example is the first Massachusetts code, the "Body of Liberties." Based extensively on English Common Law, it extended liberties in new ways toward servants, women, children, and even domestic animals. Children received recourse against parents who unreasonably denied them the freedom to marry. (Since other statutes included the death penalty for rebellious children brought by their parents before the magistrate, this represented considerable liberality of spirit.) Under the same legal code, a woman could demand a fair division of her husband's property, regardless of the stipulations of his will. And should any person "exercise any tyranny or cruelty toward any brute creature," he or she would be punishable by law.

Though, these early liberties did not extend to many freedoms we take for granted today, if Puritan leaders were unsympathetic to such basic modern American principles as religious liberty and freedom of speech, the structures they established and spiritual principles upon which they based them ultimately would facilitate liberal democratic urgings in ways they themselves could not possibly have imagined. As nineteenth-century church historian William Sweet writes in his classic, *Religion in Colonial America*, "It would be difficult to overestimate the importance of the adoption of the Congregational form of Church polity by the New England churches, in terms of the future of democracy."

To call seventeenth-century New England a theocracy—if by this one means the rule of priests—is therefore misleading. Governance rested in the hands of the congregants, not the ministerial leaders. The Mayflower Compact was drawn up wholly without benefit of clergy, the Pilgrim's pastor, John Robinson, having stayed behind in Leyden to tend the majority of his flock. Four years later, when the home church finally did dispatch a minister to the colonies, the congregation found him unsuitable and exiled him in disgrace. It was not until 1629 that a minister was settled in Plymouth.

Even then holy worship continued to be free in content and democratic in structure. This is evident from an early account drawn from Governor Winthrop's diary. In 1631, on a visit to Plymouth in the company of his minister, John Wilson, of the First Church in Boston, he describes a service far more free in form than most Protestant services today.

> On the Lord's day there was a sacrament, which they did partake in; and in the afternoon, Mr. Roger Williams propounded a question to which the pastor Mr. Smith, spoke briefly; then Mr. Williams prophesied; and then the governor of Plymouth spoke to the question; after him the elder, Brewster; then some two or three more of the congregation. Then the elder desired the governor of Massachusetts and Mr. Wilson to speak to it, which they did. When this was ended, the deacon, Mr. Fuller, put the congregation in mind of their duty of contribution;

whereupon the governor and all the rest went down to the deacon's seat, and put into the box, and then returned.

I treasure this account for several reasons. My first American ancestor, Richard Church, was surely in attendance, having moved from Boston to Plymouth shortly after his arrival in 1630. Also, First Church in Boston (now First and Second Church) was the congregation that called and ordained me into the ministry. I served there for two years while completing my doctorate at Harvard. Every day when I arrived at my office I was greeted by a statue of John Winthrop, stalwart and vital even in bronze. But far more important, Roger Williams, then a citizen of Plymouth, figures prominently in Winthrop's account of the service.

By taking what was implicit in the Puritan teachings and building upon it, Williams established the foundation for a new relationship between church and state, thus becoming the first great prophet of religious toleration in America. He based his argument on the second of the two principles mentioned above, the belief that each person stands alone before God. Underscoring the importance of individual liberty of conscience, this principle evolved from the Protestant elevation of the scriptures to a position of supreme authority. It also became the primary source for the liberal American tradition of religious tolerance and the separation of church and state.

Roger Williams's career is emblematic of America's emerging liberal and democratic spirit. Born in London in 1604, and educated at Cambridge, he arrived in Massachusetts in February 1631. Though he was only twenty-seven years old, his reputation as a fine and godly minister preceded him, and all expectations were that he would follow John Wilson as teacher of the First Church in Boston. Called to this position, he declined. A firm Separatist, he refused to serve any congregation that had not fully and emphatically severed itself from the established church. While rejecting the pomp and ceremony of the Church of England and assembling according to congregational principles, the Puritans were not Separatists. They continued to consider the Church of England as their "dear mother," a relationship Williams found intolerable.

He also had no use for Sabbath laws, and was the first American to oppose them. In November 1630, shortly before Williams arrived in Boston, a local resident by the name of John Baker was "whipped for shooting at fowl on the Sabbath day." He thus became not only the first person to be punished under the Sabbath law of the Massachusetts Bay colony but, perhaps more important, a lightning rod for Williams's campaign to strike all Sunday laws from the books. In mid-1631, Governor Winthrop wrote in his journal that "At a court holden at Boston . . . a letter was written from the court to Mr. Endicott to this effect: that Mr. Williams had declared his opinion that the magistrate might not punish the breach of the Sabbath, nor any other offense [that was religious], as it was a breach of the first table [of the Ten Commandments]." This is the kind of "meddling" that forced Williams to move from Boston.

Just as Williams burned the last of his Boston bridges, the First Church in Salem called him to serve as their teacher. Thwarted when the Boston authorities lodged a successful protest (William Bradford described him as "a man godly and zealous, having many precious parts but very unsettled in judgment"), Williams and his wife decided to move to Plymouth. There he assisted the local minister, practiced farming, and traded with the Indians.

This too would prove short-lived. Although in matters of state Williams was more a Pilgrim than a Puritan, even the Pilgrims failed to pass his rigorous test. Dissenters in England who had been persecuted by the government, upon arriving in America they ensured that the government of Plymouth Colony would remain in religious hands. This led to a collusion of church and state similar to the one they had suffered when in the minority—an irony Roger Williams could not help but point out.

Frustrated in Plymouth as he had been in Boston, and despite his own scruples and continuing reservations within the congregation, two years later, in 1633, Williams finally did take the Salem position, only to resign shortly thereafter. Again he asserted that, since they had insufficiently separated themselves from the Church of England, his conscience would not permit him to continue his association. At this point, Williams withdrew from communion with every church in New England.

Though his stay in Massachusetts was brief, Williams created a furor. This was not only due to his attitude toward Sabbath laws and his arch separatist views (extending already to an insistence on the complete separation of church and state). Williams also ran into trouble with the establishment on account of his outspoken advocacy of Indian rights. Under the charter of the Royal patent, the Massachusetts Bay Colony could seize Indian lands without remuneration, a policy he vigorously opposed. In addition, he decried the civil employment of oaths in court proceedings ("so help me God") as religious and therefore improper, and questioned the state's right both to enforce religious uniformity and to collect taxes that would go for the support of clergy.

Placed on trial in 1635, Williams was sentenced to banishment on both civil and religious grounds. With winter at its height, he set off into the wilderness, finally seeking refuge among the Indians near Narragansett Bay. That summer he purchased (rather than seized as was the custom) a parcel of their land, and founded the Providence Plantation, both providing "a shelter to persons distressed for conscience" and establishing "a civil government" that would exercise authority "only in civil things."

Other banished separatists, such as Anne Hutchinson, soon took refuge with him there. Together they created "the lively experiment" of Rhode Island, referred to by its religious detractors as "the sewer of New England." In George Bancroft's words, Roger Williams was "the first person in modern Christendom to establish a civil government on the doctrine of the liberty of conscience, the equality of opinions before the law. . . . Williams would permit persecution of no opinion, no religion, leaving heresy unharmed by law, and orthodoxy unprotected by the terrors of penal statutes."

Hitherto these statutes had been severe, and harsh punishments continued to be threatened and occasionally imposed throughout many of the other colonies long after Williams established a haven for liberty in Rhode Island. This remains the central paradox of our early history. Having fled to this country in search of religious liberty, our forebears denied this same liberty to others, often at the pain of death.

The first such statute, imposing the death penalty for blasphemy, was enacted in Virginia in 1610. It required "that no man speak impiously or maliciously, against the holy and blessed Trinity, or any of the three persons, that is to say, against God the Father, God the Son and God the Holy Ghost, or against the known articles of the Christian faith, upon pain of death." Imprisonment would follow the first offense. A second offender would "have a bodkin thrust through his tongue." Should the blasphemy occur a third time, death would follow.

In New England, some fifteen offenses called for the death penalty, including idolatry, witchcraft, blasphemy, desecration of the Sabbath, and the return of heretics after banishment. The majority of these statutes were codified in the 1640s and 1650s, shortly after Williams's trial and banishment. The most tragic chapter of religious persecution in Massachusetts took place in Salem, where "witches" were tried and sentenced to death, but other less well known instances of bigotry also darken the pages of our early history.

Among those most sorely affected were the Quakers, who first arrived in America in 1656. By 1658, the following law, concerning banishment or death "for Vagabond Quakers," was added to the Massachusetts code:

> This court doth order and enact, that every person or persons of the cursed sect of the Quakers, who is not an inhabitant of but found within this jurisdiction, shall be apprehended (without warrant) where no magistrate is at

> hand, by any constable, commissioner, or selectman, and conveyed from constable to constable until they come before the next magistrate, who shall commit the said person or persons to close prison, there to remain without bail until the next Court of Assistants where they shall have a legal trial by a special jury, and being convicted to be of the sect of the Quakers, shall be sentenced to banishment upon pain of death.

Reading the transcripts of such trials offers a reminder of how easily God's name can be invoked for diabolical ends. As Shakespeare said, even "The Devil can cite scripture for his purposes." Among recorded punishments of Quakers, the most grisly was imposed by the court of Massachusetts. First, the executioner stripped his prisoners naked from the waist up, tied them to the back of a cart, dragged them from Boston to Roxbury, and whipped them with twenty lashes along the way. There the constable repeated a like procedure, this time dragging his prisoners to Dedham, whose constable was instructed to impose the same punishment a third time. Any Quaker who still refused to recant was sentenced to death.

Three Quakers who did refuse—William Robinson, Marmaduke Stephenson, and Mary Dyer—received the death sentence in 1659. Indicating the weight of importance placed on such a conviction, the court charged Captain James Oliver to gather "one hundred soldiers, taken by his order proportionably out of each company in Boston, completely armed with pike, and musketeers, with powder and bullet" to lead the prisoners to their place of execution. There, the two men were hanged; Mary Dyer's sentence was commuted to banishment, but when she returned later, they hanged her as well.

Juridical severity against heretics was not confined to the Puritans of New England. Maryland, controlled by Catholics, imposed the death penalty and "the confiscation or forfeiture of all his or her lands and goods" on any person who failed to subscribe to the correct form of trinitarian dogma—namely the "Holy Trinity the Father Son and Holy Ghost, or the

Godhead of any of the said three Persons of the Trinity or the Unity of the Godhead." The Catholic magistrates did manage to grant limited toleration to Protestants, fearing that a "complaint may hereafter be made by them in Virginia or England" that might jeopardize Lord Baltimore's title. Even this seemed lavish just a few years later. When the Protestants assumed jurisdiction of Maryland, the Catholics, together with the Quakers, found themselves stripped of both civil and religious freedom by the Anglican establishment.

Some colonies, such as Pennsylvania and New Jersey, had far more liberal statutes, though none in the early years compared to those of Rhode Island. Though the death penalty was rarely imposed anywhere in America for such crimes as blasphemy, punishments were nonetheless severe, and continued to be imposed throughout many colonies well into the eighteenth century.

One particularly grim example is reflected in this piece of legislation passed in Delaware in 1740: "If any person shall willfully or premeditately be guilty of blasphemy, and shall thereof be legally convicted, the person so offending shall, for every such offense, be set in the pillory for the space of two hours, and be branded in his or her forehead with the letter B, and be publicly whipped, on his or her bare back, with thirty-nine lashes well laid on."

Among the chilling aspects of many of these laws is the way in which their authors tended to replace the inclusive male language customary to those times with language explicit in its reference to both men and women—a curious early example of equal treatment under law.

Reflecting on the sporadic development of religious liberty in our colonial period, colonial historian Perry Millar admits that our success in finally establishing it was somewhat accidental.

> To put it baldly, . . . we didn't aspire to freedom, we didn't march steadily toward it, we didn't unfold the inevitable propulsion of our hidden nature: we stumbled

> into it. We got a variety of sects as we got a college catalogue: the denominations and the sciences multiplied until there was nothing anybody could do about them. Wherefore we gave them permission to exist, and called the result freedom of the mind. Then we found, to our vast delight, that by thus negatively surrendering we could congratulate ourselves on a positive and heroic victory. So we stuck the feather in our cap and called it Yankee Doodle.

In large measure he is right. Religious liberty evolved as much by cultural necessity as by thoughtful argument. On the other hand, the misbegotten and ultimately futile attempts by local religious establishments to protect religion and forestall the establishment of religious liberty make Roger Williams's early experiment in tolerance and religious freedom all the more remarkable.

Roger Williams was doing a new thing in Rhode Island, a thing much more in the spirit of the scriptures than could possibly be enforced by law. It was not out of religious indifference that he favored toleration. According to his reading of the scriptures, free association and expression were essential conditions for true religious conviction. For the truth to be embraced, it must never be coerced. In Williams's view, the government is not established to enforce religion but "for the preservation of mankind in civil order and peace. The world otherwise would be like the sea, wherein men, like fishes, would hunt and devour each other, and the greater devour the less."

Roger Williams rested his defense of religious liberty on three principles: (1) All forms of religious persecution are irreligious; (2) enforced religious conformity strips belief of conviction and endangers the commonweal; and (3) both institutionally and morally, church and state are protected and thrive only when fully independent from one another. These three points constitute the framework for the liberal religious synthesis concerning church and state in America.

First, regardless of how noble the cause, any act of religious persecution countermands the teachings of Jesus. Not only is God capable of taking care of himself but any "ends justify the means" effort to impose religious teachings, however true those teachings may be, undermines the gospel.

Williams's graphic term for religious persecution was "rape of the soul." When people are forced to believe what they do not, the conscience is ravished and Christ's message is violated. Citing the parable of the wheat and the tares in Matthew 13, Williams insisted that the tares (ingenerate Christians or infidels) not be molested; this would only jeopardize the wheat growing in their midst. On Judgment Day, God would separate the two, harvesting the wheat and burning the tares. Before this harvest, any human attempt to divide wheat from tares would surely prove premature, haphazard, and self-defeating.

Second, since salvation cannot be coerced, each individual must be permitted the full latitude of his or her conscience in all private matters, especially with respect to religion. Williams offered two reasons for this, one positive and one negative: (1) Religion cannot be authentic without liberty; and (2) those who enforce their own beliefs on another may be wrong. When possessed by falsehood, those prosecuting the truth become persecutors of the truth, crucifiers in Christ's name. Williams's insistence on liberty of conscience, with its corollary, tolerance toward those with unpopular opinions, is the keystone for all subsequent legislation protecting minority rights, whether religious, social, or political. In Williams's view, the civil authorities must "provide in their high wisdom for the security of all the respective meetings, assemblings, worshippings, preaching, disputings, etc . . . [so] that civil peace and the beauty of civility and humanity [may] be maintained among the chief opposers and dissenters."

This proposition undergirds Williams's third argument in favor of religious liberty: It is in the best interest of both church and state for the two to remain independent. To begin with, he could find no warrant in scripture for any such collusion.

> I observed the great and wonderful mistake, both our own and our fathers, as to the civil powers of this world, acting in spiritual matters. I have read . . . the last will and testament of the Lord Jesus over many times, and yet I cannot find by one tittle of that testament that if He had been pleased to have accepted of a temporal crown and government that ever He would have put forth the least finger of temporal or civil power in the matters of His spiritual affairs and Kingdom. Hence must it lamentably be against the testimony of Christ Jesus for the civil state to impose upon the souls of the people a religion, a worship, a ministry, oaths (in religious and civil affairs), tithes, times, days, marryings, and buryings in holy ground.

Freed to make his own distinctions between religious and secular authority, Williams proceeded to distinguish between the two tables of the Decalogue (the Ten Commandments given by God to Moses on Mt. Sinai). The first table concerns our relationship with God. Such matters fall outside secular jurisdiction. This affects any statute regarding blasphemy, heresy, or Sunday observance. The laws from the second table concern our relationship with our neighbors. Williams considered these not only to be religious laws but also "the law of nature, the law moral and civil," applicable to all regardless of faith, and constituting the basis for public morality. Accordingly, such laws must be enforced not by religious but by secular magistrates. Not only that, but the magistrates need not be Christian in order to adjudicate them rightly, for being Christian bestows no special advantage when it comes to questions of natural law. As Williams himself put it:

> There is a moral virtue, a moral fidelity, ability, and honesty, which other men (beside Church-members) are, by

> good nature and education, by good laws and good examples nourished and trained up in, that civil places need not be monopolized into the hands of Church-members (who sometimes are not fitted for them), and all others deprived of their natural and civil rights and liberties.

With this innovation (inspired by the scriptures) a fundamental shift takes place. No longer is the colony—and later the nation—a Christian colony, for the government is no longer a Christian government.

On religious, not secular grounds, Roger Williams thus established the basis for American pluralism, a position he expressed succinctly in this exchange with John Cotton, John Wilson's colleague in the ministry at Boston's First Church and a spirited defender of established religion in Massachusetts. Cotton claimed that "No good Christian, much less a good magistrate, can be ignorant of the Principles of saving truth." Williams replied, "This assertion, confounding the nature of civil and moral goodness with religious, is as far from goodness, as darkness is from light."

Roger Williams's legacy is etched clearly in the early records of Rhode Island. The Providence Compact of 1636 explicitly states that all laws to be enacted for the public good would obtain only with respect to "civil things," not religious. In 1640, the Providence Plantation agreement affirms, "As formerly hath been the liberties of the town, so still, to hold forth liberty of conscience."

In 1643, Roger Williams traveled to England to secure a charter for Rhode Island, coupled with explicit assurances of protection against any interference in its affairs by the Puritans of Massachusetts. Four years later, the Rhode Island General Assembly drew up a code of laws, culminating in the famous religious liberty clause, granting that "All men may walk as their consciences persuade them, everyone in the name of his God . . . without molestation."

In 1774, just before the American Revolution, a new Baptist

church was built in Providence. The following year they dedicated their bell, having first engraved on it the following inscription:

> For freedom of conscience, the town was first planted,
> Persuasion, not force, was used by the people.
> This church is the eldest, and has not recanted,
> Enjoying and granting, bell, temple, and steeple.

A telling yet harmonious variation on the Liberty Bell motto ("Proclaim liberty throughout all the land unto all the inhabitants thereof"), both were inspired by a religious spirit sufficiently broad to ensure civil liberty, not to some but to all. This is the spirit of Roger Williams, a true Baptist, who called for "soul freedom," and fought for liberty.

# 5

# *We Hold These Truths*

> As Mankind become more liberal, they will be more apt to allow that all those who conduct themselves as worthy members of the community are equally entitled to the protections of civil government. I hope ever to see America among the foremost nations in examples of justice and liberality.
>
> —GEORGE WASHINGTON

SCHOLARS SEEK TO SEPARATE the man from the myth, but at one level the myth matters more. Truth-teller; citizen-soldier; reluctant leader who esteemed his country's needs above his own; devoted husband; teacher of children; square-jawed; independent-minded; gentle-hearted; unutterably wise; and possessed of a generous spirit: George Washington stands together with our flag, Liberty Bell, Statue of Liberty, and Declaration of Independence as one of this nation's most evocative and inspirational icons.

The story of a boy holding an axe next to a fallen cherry tree while confessing to his father "I cannot tell a lie" has surely inspired as much youthful truth-telling as any in our national canon. That he was a far better president than general (in sharp contrast to Ulysses S. Grant and Dwight David Eisenhower) subtracts nothing from the stirring image of a wind-blown hero standing in a tiny boat spiriting his men across the Delaware. Nor should we care that his classic jaw resulted from a bad set of wooden false teeth, or even that his fidelity to Martha may well have been exaggerated.

On the other hand, given the power we invest in his image, it does matter that Washington's beliefs not be misrepresented. Anyone who cashes in on "the father of our country" to advance narrow, sectarian values desecrates his memory and our history. The truth is that George Washington, together with Thomas Jefferson and James Madison, should rank near the top of anybody's list of famous liberals.

Here we *could* do with a few facts. Given the recent upsurge of religious bigotry, Washington's oft-stated concern that "Of all the animosities which have existed among mankind, those which are caused by a difference of sentiments in religion appear to be the most inveterate and distressing, and ought most to be deprecated" is prescient. He was referring to his own neighbors. Upon leaving office, Washington's deepest regret concerned sectarian Christian rivalries. Invoking the liberal spirit (Washington employed the L word more often than any of our founders), he sadly confessed, "I was in hopes, that the enlightened and liberal policy, which has marked the present age, would at least have reconciled *Christians* of every denomination so far, that we should never again see their religious disputes carried to such a pitch as to endanger the peace of society." In this respect, he stands at the source spring of our experiment in freedom and democracy, and should be numbered not only among our nation's founders but also among its most avid protectors. As one early biographer put it, "As long as the ideals and principles championed by George Washington hold a dominant place in the hearts of the American people, religious liberty will remain secure."

During his term as president, Washington penned numerous letters to Catholics, Jews, and Protestant sectarians, confirming their rights of conscience. To the General Committee representing the United Baptist Churches in Virginia, he wrote that "Every man, conducting himself as a good citizen, and being accountable alone to God for his religious opinion, ought to be protected in worshipping the Deity according to the dictates of his own conscience." There is nothing perfunctory here. Washington was worried.

> If I could have entertained the slightest apprehension, that the constitution framed in the convention, where I had the honor to preside, might possibly endanger the religious rights of any ecclesiastical society, certainly I would never have placed my signature to it; and, if I could now conceive that the general government might ever be so administered as to render the liberty of conscience insecure, I beg you will be persuaded, that no one would be more zealous than myself to establish effectual barriers against the horrors of spiritual tyranny, and every species of religious persecution.

Selected from many that could establish the same point, this passage answers anyone who would dare extrapolate dogmatic intentions from the liberal faith of our nation's founders. Washington honored religious liberty (which cannot be severed from the separation of church and state) foremost among our rights. His greatest disappointment was that many of the states were slow in following the federal example to ban religious discrimination, persecution, and privilege.

Those who argue that Washington, or the senators who ratified the early treaties, considered the United States a "Christian" nation in any other than a descriptive sense need look no farther than the language contained in these early treaties. To give but a single example, the eleventh article of a 1795 treaty with Tripoli states this clearly:

> As the Government of the United States of America is not in any sense founded on the Christian Religion; as it has in itself no character of enmity against the laws, religion, or tranquillity of Musselmen; and as the said States never have entered into any war or act of hostility against any Mehomitan nation, it is declared by the parties, that no pretext arising from religious opinions shall ever produce

an interruption of the harmony existing between the two countries.

On the other hand, almost all of our founding fathers viewed their life and work in a broad religious frame. George Washington was not devout, but he did attend Christian services on a regular basis, and esteemed religion as central to our communal life as a nation. As with many of our presidents, Washington practiced civil religion: "One nation under God, indivisible, with liberty and justice for all."

Some consider civil religion a thin broth, without religious substance. Others recoil from it, even in its most formulaic expression, as an unconscionable abridgment of the First Amendment. Washington would have found both sides of this debate baffling. I can't imagine him troubling himself, one way or another, with recitation of the Pledge of Allegiance in our public schools. Nor would the decision to inscribe the words "In God We Trust" on our currency have cost him any sleep. However staunch in his advocacy of church-state separation, Washington would have viewed "In God We Trust" or "One nation under God" not as dangerous abridgments of needful separation but rather as chastening reminders, encouragements to humility, recalling us to the limitations of our power.

However ubiquitous, neither phrase prompts much serious reflection these days. Perhaps they should. As inscribed on our currency, the words "In God We Trust" remind us where to place (and not to place) our faith. Every bill in our wallet and coin in our pocket says, "Don't trust in me. Trust and believe in something higher. Otherwise you will lapse into idolatry, with mammon as your God." Jesus taught us to render unto Caesar only what was Caesar's. What better way to remain mindful of the limit to "Caesar's" rightful claim than to imprint on every bill and coin "In God We Trust."

By the same token, in the Pledge of Allegiance, our nation is not over God; it is under God. We live under, not beyond, judgment. It may be tempting to claim that God is on our side, but we can't. God is above us, a higher sovereignty than any officers of our republic (or our churches) can arrogate either for themselves or their ideas.

One fundamental difference between democracy and authoritarianism or totalitarianism is that the latter forms of governance (even atheistic ones) submit themselves more easily to religious idolatries—where the part is worshiped in place of the whole. If "God" symbolizes the highest power and value we know, almost all monarchs and tyrants end up playing God. Their word is law, and their decrees final; they brook no insolence, dissent, or disrespect. "In Caesar We Trust," the coins say; "One nation under Caesar," reads the Pledge of Allegiance. So long as we understand the word *God* in as broad, inclusive, and nonsectarian a sense as our founders did, references to God on our currency or in our pledge put the lie to all such hubris. Whether political or religious, our leaders are not gods, not even demigods. Despite the squeamishness of atheists, far from polluting our commerce with religion, an expressed trust in nature's God underpins the principles of democracy.

The same holds with our Pledge of Allegiance: We don't swear fidelity to the United States of America *über alles* (above all); we pledge allegiance to one nation "under" God. As President Vaclav Havel of Czechoslovakia reminded the American Congress in late 1989, "The salvation of this human world lies nowhere else than in human responsibility. . . . Responsibility to something higher than my family, my country, my company, my success—responsibility to the order of being where all our actions are indelibly recorded and where and only where they will be properly judged." These words are inspired by and spoken in the true religious spirit of our nation's founders.

Since the word *God* comes packed with the freight of whoever utters it, some people suggest that we should banish *God* from all public discourse. I held the same position for years. And there is reason for wariness. Certain groups on the religious right claim that since the authors of our Declaration of

Independence and Constitution were Christians, both documents are Christian in intention and should be interpreted accordingly. I heard one minister corroborate this claim (on the Morton Downey, Jr., Show no less) by citing the closing words of the Constitution: "Anno Domini 1787" ("In the year of our Lord, 1787"). "Who is our Lord," he asked rhetorically, "if not the savior and Messiah, Jesus Christ."

Rightfully offended by such specious, sophistical rhetoric, others argue that Christianity is not even implicit in these texts. I sympathize with their outrage, but the truth lies somewhere in-between. If clearly not sectarian, our foundational documents do evince a religious attitude, universalist in scope and liberal in intent.

The United States of America is a religious nation, founded on liberal religious principles. These principles derive primarily from considered and practical reflection on two texts, the Bible and the creation: the former mediated through Puritan polity and Reformation doctrine concerning individual rights of conscience; the latter interpreted by Enlightenment thinkers attempting to establish a just society on the divine foundation of nature and nature's God.

Nowhere is this more evident than in the Declaration of Independence. Invoking "the laws of nature and nature's God" to confirm as every people's entitlement a "separate and equal station," Thomas Jefferson expands the notion of equality from a people, or nation, to all persons: "We hold these truths to be self-evident, that all men are created equal, that they are endowed by their Creator with certain unalienable rights, that among these are life, liberty, and the pursuit of happiness."

Revisionist historians rightly point out that "all men" did not include either women or slaves. Yet, despite Jefferson's human limitations and the common presuppositions of the society in which he lived, his words in the preamble of our Declaration of Independence do establish an ideal of equity and liberty for all. Cynics may dismiss this as pious rhetoric, but, taken seriously, it is actually rhetoric conducive to piety. Drawing from a theology based on the notion of natural right, he argued that a just and fair society would imitate, not countermand, the laws of nature's God. As he perceived them, these laws are just because God is righteous, and fair because God is good.

Even Alexander Hamilton, Jefferson's conservative counterpart, wrote that our God-given rights "are not to be rummaged for among old parchments and musty records. They are written, as with a sunbeam, in the whole *volume* of human nature, by the hand of divinity itself, and can never be erased or obscured by mortal power." Elsewhere, Hamilton explicitly links civil to natural law: "Natural liberty is a gift of the beneficent Creator, to the whole human race and . . . civil liberty is founded on that and cannot be wrested from any people without the most manifest violation of justice."

By the late eighteenth century, both Puritans and Enlightenment thinkers, democrats as well as federalists, accepted this broad formula. The distinctions lay primarily in emphasis. Is it more important to protect the individual from society, or society from the individual? Are minorities more threatened by the majority, or vice versa? In practice, basic principles such as equality and liberty often conflict; in theory, they complement one another.

John Locke's view of liberty, established in the context of natural law, couples freedom with duty. Placing a fundamental restriction on each person's liberty, namely that it not impinge on the liberty of another, tempers the excesses of possessive individualism. In this sense, the laissez-faire, or dog-eat-dog, economic liberalism of the nineteenth century—the very "liberalism" nostalgically celebrated by many of today's neoconservatives—contradicts the liberalism of our founders.

Even the Constitution provides for "public welfare" as well as public safety. Regarding self-love, or the principle of untrammeled libertarianism, Jefferson wrote that it "is no part of morality. . . . It is the sole antagonist of virtue, leading us constantly by our propensities to self-gratification in violation of our moral duties to others. . . . Nature hath implanted in our breasts a love of others, a sense of duty to them, a moral instinct, in short, which prompts us irresistibly to feel and to succor their distresses."

The liberal tradition of Locke and Jefferson rests on responsibility, not cupidity. Jefferson struck this chord in his first inaugural address, leading with an appeal for "Equal and exact justice to all men, of whatever state or persuasion." Anyone who doubts his sincerity might note that, later, with respect to the continuing establishment of slavery, he went on to say, "Indeed I tremble for my country when I reflect that God is just; that his justice cannot sleep forever."

Any attempt to rekindle the liberal spirit in America begins here. Instead of backing away from a vigorous prosecution of minority rights in order to placate a self-interested majority, we must rekindle the spirit of our founders at their best. As emblazoned on the pages of the Declaration of Independence and the Bill of Rights, this is both a moral and a religious charge.

Removed from its foundation in natural theology, the principle of equality of opportunity is reduced to social Darwinism—the economic survival of the fittest. Instead of a cooperative social ethic, facilitated by law to promote the cultivation of every individual's promise and to protect every individual's rights, self-interested individualism emerges as our model, often draped with patriotic bunting ripped from the fabric of such documents as the Declaration of Independence and the Constitution. This misrepresents not only Jefferson but also John Locke. Both believed that the liberty of one person has neither ethical nor political validity apart from the protection of others' liberty.

The litmus test for democratic societies is not the number of liberties offered but the number of people to whom they are offered, and the extent to which these liberties are protected. Without such protection under law, individual liberty undermines liberal democracy, which devolves into a de facto tyranny of the privileged few over the many. Liberty untempered by equity is immoral. It violates both the Bible and the book of nature's God.

In May 1761, preaching before the Great and General Court of Massachusetts, the Rev. Benjamin Stevens proclaimed that civil liberty stems directly from natural liberty, as interpreted by the spirit of Christ, and established to ensure "the safety and happiness of the people." In 1775, John Adams echoed the same point, a commonplace of the time, in a letter to George Wythe: "The happiness of society is the end of government, as all divine and moral philosophers will agree that the happiness of the individual is the end of man. From this principle it will follow that the form of government which communicates ease, comfort, security or, in one word, happiness, to the greatest number of persons, and in the greatest degree, is the best."

Ironically, this same principle, "the pursuit of happiness," codified in our Declaration of Independence as an unalienable right, today forms the trip wire for many who cite our founders as authorities to legitimate their overweening reverence for unbridled liberty. And indeed, stripped of its philosophical and theological content, it can easily be mistaken as a license for individual self-aggrandizement.

The word *pursuit* suggests a race or a quest. *Happiness*, at least according to the corporate manipulators of the American spirit, is a state of well-being, best measured according to one's accumulation of material possessions. As promulgated both by television sit-coms and the advertisements that support them, happiness is the right imported vodka, a red Japanese convertible, hot sex, cool clothes, and yearly vacations in the Caribbean. By this script, for the government to impinge on our freedom to grab is un-American, especially when it comes to paying taxes to underwrite the indolence of our unproductive and therefore less deserving neighbors.

American liberalism is perverted when it lapses into either libertinism or libertarianism. Idolatries of freedom enshrine liberty as an unholy sacred cow, predicating happiness on the principle of self-gratification or self-interest. In biblical parlance, idolatry results when something less than God (even something good) is worshiped as, or in the place of, God. When worshiped apart from other goods, such as justice and neighborliness, even so noble a principle as freedom can have a corrosive effect.

Contemporary conservatives leap to associate liberalism with its excesses, blaming our overweening devotion to liberty for the breakdown in values and the unraveling of our societal fabric. Simultaneously they champion and rarely criticize the very corporations most responsible for firing our desires and whetting our appetites, turning wants into needs, reducing happiness to self-gratification, and offering enticements by which, at tremendous cost both to our pocketbooks and our souls, such happiness can be purchased. The so-called excesses of liberalism are induced far more effectively by the conservative champions of free-market corporate America than they are by the Civil Liberties Union.

When they spoke of the pursuit of happiness, our liberal founders had something more redemptive in mind than mere self-gratification or self-aggrandizement. They thought of it as a divine right, with attending moral consequences. In his *Commentaries on the Laws of England* published in the late 1760s, influential jurist William Blackstone offers perhaps the most complete definition of happiness as understood in the context of natural law. Speaking of "those rights, . . . which God and nature have established, and are therefore called natural rights, such as are life and liberty," Blackstone places happiness first: " 'That man should pursue his own happiness' . . . is the foundation of what we call ethics, or natural law." One important condition is attached. "[The Creator] has so intimately connected, so inseparably interwoven the laws of eternal justice with the happiness of each individual, that the latter cannot be attained but by observing the former; and, if the former be punctually obeyed, it cannot but induce the latter."

By this reading, pursuit is a vocation or calling, not a chase, and happiness is an attainment of the good, not of goods. George Washington said it in his First Inaugural Address: "There is no truth more thoroughly established than that there exists in the economy and course of nature an indissoluble union between virtue and happiness; between duty and advantage; between the genuine maxims of an honest and magnanimous policy and the solid rewards of public prosperity and felicity." He adds a warning. "We ought to be no less persuaded that the propitious smiles of Heaven can never be expected on a nation that disregards the eternal rules of order and right which Heaven itself has ordained."

For John Locke, the trilogy of self-evident rights was "life, liberty, and property." The importance of Jefferson's substitution of happiness for property in the American Declaration of Independence cannot be overestimated. As we have seen from Blackstone's *Commentaries*, and could demonstrate by reference to many other contemporary sources—from the writings of jurist Jean Jacques Burlamaqui to those of Scottish moral philosopher Francis Hutcheson—this innovation is hardly original with Jefferson. Yet, in terms of the development of liberal democratic thought, it is momentous. Neither Jefferson nor his philosophical predecessors viewed happiness through the lens of individualism. Hutcheson, a Presbyterian minister, framed it as "That action is best which accomplishes the greatest happiness for the greatest number." Citing Hutcheson's influence, Garry Wills writes that "When Jefferson spoke of pursuing happiness, he had nothing vague or private in mind. He meant a public happiness which is measurable; which is, indeed, the test and justification of any government."

In the Virginia Bill of Rights, which preceded the Declaration of Independence, the rights of life and liberty are coupled with "the means of acquiring and possessing property, and pursuing and obtaining happiness and safety." Jefferson's decision to drop the narrower right of property and sum both up in the single phrase, the pursuit of happiness, indicates the universalizing tendency of liberalism.

This tendency leads critics to brand liberals as either hypocrites or dreamers. And not without justification: Liberal rhetoric and reality often conflict.

Consider this famous husband-wife exchange from early U.S. history. Abigail Adams wrote a letter to her husband John requesting that, in helping to draw up a new code of laws, he "would remember the ladies and be more generous and favorable to them than your ancestors."

In practice, the results were not more favorable. Such contradictions invite cynicism. That cynicism is understandable, but when liberals liberate themselves from failed policies, the spirit of liberalism has a regenerative quality. By definition, liberalism is open-ended and self-critical. Responding to his wife, Adams admitted, "New claims will arise; women will demand a vote . . . and every man who has not a farthing, will demand an equal vote with any other, in all acts of state." As with Jefferson and slavery, Adams was not ready to act unilaterally to right an injustice. But he did recognize that those who followed would one day challenge the inequality of male and female, as well as that of rich and poor. The liberal spirit of the Declaration of Independence—its stress on the God-given rights of equality, liberty, and the pursuit of happiness—provides latter-day American champions of women's and minority rights with a patriotic blueprint for their own prophetic work.

If the pursuit of happiness is an inalienable right granted by the creator, another gloss on its meaning can be found in the scriptures. In the King James version of the Old Testament, the words *happiness* or *happy* occur only seventeen times, but in each instance the occurrence is as an ethical not a material attainment. Happy are those who live according to God's precepts, not those who die with the most toys.

A striking juxtaposition between happiness and morality occurs in the French translation of the Beatitudes (which Thomas Jefferson kept by his bedside). The word we render as *blessed*, the French translate as *heureux* or happy.

Happy are the poor in spirit, for theirs is the kingdom of heaven.
Happy are those who mourn, for they shall be comforted.
Happy are the meek, for they shall inherit the earth.
Happy are those who hunger and thirst for righteousness, for they shall be satisfied.

Happy are the merciful, for they shall obtain mercy.
Happy are the pure in heart, for they shall see God.
Happy are the peacemakers, for they shall be called the children of God.
Happy are those who are persecuted for righteousness' sake, for theirs is the kingdom of heaven.

Coupling the Prologue of the Declaration of Independence to the Beatitudes of Jesus may stretch our founders' intentions, but they would not have been startled or disappointed to find the two framed together. Less than a month before the Declaration of Independence, when Virginia passed its own Declaration of Rights, the final two sections, written by Patrick Henry and amended by James Madison, explicitly couple the political principles of liberty and equality with the exercise of biblical virtues such as justice and mercy.

> Section 15. That no free government, or the blessings of liberty, can be preserved to any people but by a firm adherence to justice, moderation, temperance, frugality, and virtue, and by frequent recurrence to fundamental principles.
>
> Section 16. That religion, or the duty which we owe to our Creator, and the manner of discharging it, can be directed only by reason and conviction, not by force or violence; and, therefore, all men are equally entitled to the free exercise of religion, according to the dictates of conscience; and that it is the mutual duty of all to practice Christian forbearance, love, and charity towards each other.

Even as the first section of the Virginia Declaration of Rights suggested the language of the propositional clause in the Declaration of Independence ("life, liberty, and the pursuit of happiness"), the sixteenth section anticipates the First Amendment of the Bill of Rights.

An illustrative anecdote comes from the colorful pages of late colonial Virginia history. However inconsistent in his application of the principle, no one was more passionate in his defense of religious liberty than Patrick Henry. The greatest speaker of his day, Henry regularly lent his rhetorical and legal talents to those apprehended for breaking religious statutes. And not only religious ones: From 1768 to 1775 Baptist ministers in Virginia were often cited for violating the more general secular law against "disturbing the peace."

On one such occasion, Patrick Henry rode fifty miles to plead the case for several Baptist ministers. He arrived late, entering the courtroom just as the prosecuting attorney was reading the indictment. Slightly out of breath, Henry rose and in a halting manner, as if unable to comprehend what he had just heard, expressed his bewilderment. "May it please the court, what did I hear read? Did I hear it distinctly, or was it a mistake of my own? Did I hear an expression as of crime, that these men, whom your Worships are about to try for misdemeanor, are charged with—with—with what?" As if the enormity of the charge were too great to be spoken aloud, Henry then whispered the answer: "Preaching the gospel of the Son of God!" Henry rolled his eyes, lifted his hands above his head, and thundered, "Great God!" His voice dripping with irony, he then asked the court:

> May it please your Worships, in a day like this, when Truth is about to burst her fetters; when mankind are about to be aroused to claim their natural and inalienable rights; when the yoke of oppression that has reached the wilderness of America, and the unnatural alliance of ecclesiastical and civil power is about to be dissevered—at *such* a period, when Liberty, Liberty of Conscience, is about to wake from her slumberings, . . . these people are accused of *preaching the gospel of the Son of God*?

Again he lifted his eyes to heaven, gasped "Great God!" and concluded his brief by launching a telling, if romanticized, precis of American history: "From that period when our fathers left the land of their nativity for these American wilds, . . . from that moment despotism was crushed, the fetters of darkness were broken, and Heaven decreed that man should be free. . . . In vain were all their offerings and bloodshed to subjugate this new world, if we, their offspring, must still be oppressed and persecuted." Patrick Henry shook his head, lowered his voice, and asked, "May it please your Worships, permit me to inquire once more, For what are these men about to be tried? This paper says, *for preaching the gospel of the Savior to Adam's fallen race*!"

As Patrick Henry sat down, the presiding judge called a halt to the proceedings. "Sheriff," he said solemnly, "discharge these men."

If capable of rising to rhetorical heights on behalf of religious liberty, Patrick Henry fell short of being a completely adequate philosopher of rights. In his original draft of the sixteenth section of the Virginia Declaration of Rights, the wording read that "All men should enjoy the fullest toleration in the exercise of religion, according to the dictates of conscience." James Madison vigorously objected to this phrasing. The free exercise of religion was a right, not a privilege. Privileges can be removed by governments; rights are established in natural law.

Tolerance is a condescending virtue. When it comes to the rights of conscience, respect is called for, not mere tolerance. In his debate with Patrick Henry, James Madison prevailed, changing the wording to read "All men are equally *entitled* to the free exercise of religion, according to the dictates of conscience."

More conventionally religious than Jefferson, Madison was a practicing churchman, an active Anglican, and a devout Christian. At Princeton, under the tutelage of John Witherspoon, he undertook a serious study of religion, concentrating on theology and biblical studies. A staunch Presbyterian, Witherspoon inspired Madison with a passion for Christian orthodoxy and religious liberty. After leaving Princeton, until political events called him to a life of public service, Madison continued to pursue his study of theology.

He fought his first extended political battle on behalf of religious liberty in Virginia. Among his staunchest allies in this long, bitter struggle were Presbyterians. As early as 1776, the Presbytery of Hanover filed a Dissenter's Petition with the Virginia General Assembly, invoking the spirit of the Virginia Declaration of Rights' call for the "free exercise of Religion according to the dictates of our Consciences," and requesting that all citizens of Virginia be free from a levy, tax, or any imposition whatsoever collected on behalf of the established church, the Church of England. In the words of their petition, "To judge for ourselves, and to engage in the exercise of religion agreeable to the dictates of our own Consciences, is an unalienable right, which, upon the principles that the Gospel was first propagated, . . . can never be transferred to another."

Adding religious freedom of conscience to the inalienable rights of life, liberty, and the pursuit of happiness, these believers testified both to the theological and political importance of this principle. Madison took up the refrain:

> The religion then of every man must be left to the conviction and conscience of every man; and it is the right of every man to exercise it as these may dictate. This right is in its nature an unalienable right. It is unalienable; because the opinions of men, depending only on the evidence contemplated by their own minds, cannot follow the dictates of other men: It is unalienable also; because what is here a right toward men, is a duty towards the Creator. It is the duty of every man to render to the Creator such homage, and such only, as he believes to be acceptable to Him.

Over the nine years before this "unalienable right" would be granted under law, nearly every other nonestablished religious body in Virginia followed the Presbyterians' lead. Virginia's secretary of state testified to the power of their grassroots effort, noting that "Numbers of petitions, memorials, etc., in manuscript are on file in the archives here from religious bodies of almost every denomination, from nearly every county in this State, during the period of the Revolution."

Yet, such was the power of the established church to protect the status quo that the legislature proved resistant. In 1784, when support for the establishment began to wane, Patrick Henry proposed a compromise bill favoring a general tax for the support of religion, hoping that by including religious sectaries in the public largess, they would finally desist in their attempts to subvert public religious financing. (Though opposed to all statutes restricting religious freedom, Henry remained unconvinced that the church could thrive without state assistance.) Henry's bill provided that each person could designate the church to which his or her taxes would be sent.

Madison offered a compromise that would place the question of religious assessments up for a vote, letting the people decide. Certain that he would prevail at the polls, Henry agreed. He was mistaken. Years later in a letter to General Lafayette, Madison described his victory in these words:

> In the year 1785, a bill was introduced under the auspices of Mr. Henry, imposing a general tax for the support of "Teachers of the Christian Religion." It made a progress, threatening a majority in its favor. As an expedient to defeat it, we proposed that it should be postponed to another session, and printed in the meantime for public consideration. Such an appeal in a case so important and so unforeseen could not be resisted. With a view to arouse the people, it was thought proper that a memorial [petition] should be drawn up, the task being assigned to me, to be printed and circulated through the State for a general signature. The experiment succeeded. The memorial was so extensively signed, by the various religious sects, including a considerable portion of the old hierarchy, that the projected innovation was crushed, and under the influence of the popular sentiment thus called forth, the well-

> known bill prepared by Mr. Jefferson, for "establishing religious freedom," passed into a law, as it now stands in our Code of Statutes.

Jefferson considered the "Act for Establishing Religious Freedom in Virginia" to be one of his three most abiding public accomplishments, listing it, together with his authorship of the Declaration of Independence and founding of the University of Virginia—but not his eight years as president of the United States—on his tombstone at Monticello. Following in the spirit of the Virginia Bill of Rights and Declaration of Independence, and anticipating the First Amendment of the Bill of Rights, this act is central to the establishment and preservation of our liberal democracy. Jefferson feared that "the spirit of the times may alter, will alter. Our rulers will become corrupt, our people careless. A single zealot may commence persecution, and better men be his victims." For this reason, together with Madison he struggled assiduously to confirm basic rights, such as religious freedom of conscience, as the law of the land.

As he would later in the Declaration of Independence, in his Act for Establishing Religious Freedom in Virginia, Jefferson based his argument on a foundation of natural law:

> Whereas Almighty God hath created the mind free; that all attempts to influence it by temporal punishments or burthens, or by civil incapacitations, tend only to beget habits of hypocrisy and meanness, and are a departure from the plan of the Holy Author of our religion, who being Lord both of body and mind, yet chose not to propagate it by coercions on either. . . . *Be it enacted by the General Assembly*, That no man shall be compelled to frequent or support any religious worship, place, or ministry whatsoever, nor shall be enforced, restrained, molested, or burthened in his body or goods, nor shall otherwise suffer on account of his religious opinions or belief; but that all men shall be free to profess, and by ar-

gument to maintain, their opinion in matters of religion, and that the same shall in no wise diminish, enlarge, or affect their civil capacities.

The separation of church and state is America's most distinctive contribution to modern statecraft. First championed by Roger Williams, then developed and codified by James Madison and Thomas Jefferson, this wall protects religion and religious practice more than it restricts them. But to secure our freedoms, one thing remained. Laws already on the books in Rhode Island, Virginia, Pennsylvania, and New Jersey must become the law of the land.

When the first Congress convened in 1789, James Madison moved to promote legislation that would append to the new constitution a supplemental Bill of Rights. In the first draft of the Bill of Rights, what we know as the First Amendment came third, after one guaranteeing congressional representation to every 50,000 citizens, and another stating that Congress could not receive a voted raise in salary until the people had an opportunity in the next election to throw the rascals out. The latter issue continues to bedevil Congress; the former, if enacted, would mandate, according to our present population, a House of Representatives with 4,400 members. Both amendments failed to elicit the two-thirds vote necessary for ratification, permitting the one establishing our basic freedoms to assume its natural place, that of primacy among the ten amendments that constitute our Bill of Rights.

In the congressional debate over the Bill of Rights, devoted to the principle that freedom of religion, press, and speech be explicitly guaranteed under law, James Madison disputed those who believed that such provisions were either unnecessary or counterproductive. To the former, who argued that such rights existed in natural law and needed no provision under civil law to ensure their enforcement, he pointed to history. Without protection, religious minorities remain at the mercy of whatever religious establishment may dominate in any given age. As his compatriot Jefferson wrote years later to

Rabbi Mordecai M. Noah, "Your sect by its sufferings has furnished a remarkable proof of the universal spirit of religious intolerance, inherent in every sect, disclaimed by all while feeble, and practised by all when in power. . . . Public opinion erects itself into an Inquisition, and exercises its office with as much fanaticism as fans the flames of an *auto da fe*."

Madison and Jefferson designed the first amendment as a necessary, if not sufficient, wall to protect the government from religion *and* religious minorities from a government responsive to the religious demands of those in the majority. The clauses regarding religion in the Bill of Rights suggest no hostility to religion, nor do they sever religious from legal values. They insist only that the government not impose any single code of religious teaching on the members of a pluralistic society.

It is a question of balance. Those who dismiss the spiritual foundations of our republic cannot be relied on to ensure and protect the principles upon which this nation was founded: biblical teachings concerning equity, justice, mercy, and humility; and the broader religious conviction that all are created equal and endowed by their creator with certain unalienable rights (life, liberty, the pursuit of happiness, and religious freedom of conscience). On the other hand, those who impose a doctrinal understanding of Christianity on the Declaration of Independence and Constitution misread and subvert the intentions of our nation's architects.

This is a religious country. To the extent that it is christian, it is christian with a small "c." The christian spirit of the authors and architects of our republic is supplemented by and mediated through Enlightenment thought, which, though religious, is universalist (catholic with a small "c") in spirit, transcending and wary of all forms of sectarianism. Even the specifically Christian principles that undergird our nation, first established in Puritan polity and doctrine, and then purified in practice by such pioneers as Roger Williams and William Penn, point to a division between the laws of the church and the laws that govern society.

How can we balance the two? As American church historian Robert Handy once asked, "Can a nation retain both full religious freedom and a particular religious character?"

George Washington, Thomas Jefferson, and James Madison could have answered easily. When the particular religious character of a nation is predicated on the principle of religious freedom, if we continue to honor that principle, the answer is "Yes."

# 6

# *One Nation Under God*

The shepherd drives the wolf from the sheep's throat, for which the sheep thanks the shepherd as a liberator, while the wolf denounces him for the same act as the destroyer of liberty; especially as the sheep was a black one. Plainly the sheep and the wolf are not agreed on a definition of the word liberty.

—Abraham Lincoln

On February 3, 1863, during one of the darkest months of our nation's history, representatives from eleven Protestant denominations gathered at a convention in Xenia, Ohio, to establish the National Reform Association. Their agenda had nothing to do with the abolition of slavery. These Christian gentlemen instead shared a commitment to defend Bible reading in the public schools; extend existing Sabbath legislation; protect the American family from corruption; resist all attempts to abolish Christian oaths or prayer in our national and state legislatures; ensure the continuance of national days of fasting and thanksgiving; and prohibit the legal sale of liquor.

They chose to accomplish these pious aims by means of a constitutional amendment. It would explicitly proclaim "the nation's allegiance to Jesus Christ and its acceptance of the moral laws of the Christian religion, and so indicate that this is a Christian nation, and place all the Christian laws, institutions, and usages of our government on an undeniably legal basis in the fundamental law of the land." Worried that the lack of any specifically Christian reference in the Constitution undercut its moral authority and thwarted honest Christian attempts to legislate God's law, they proposed the following amendment:

> We, the people of the United States, [humbly acknowledging Almighty God as the source of all authority and power in civil government, the Lord Jesus Christ as the Ruler among the nations, His revealed will as the supreme law of the land, in order to constitute a Christian government,] and in order to form a more perfect union . . . do ordain and establish this Constitution for the United States of America.

A prototype of Jerry Falwell's Moral Majority, the National Reform movement grew rapidly, its influence extending well into the twentieth century. Regarding constitutional guaranties for freedom of conscience as a "dangerous weapon" in the hands of secularists, their goal was to "furnish an undeniably legal basis for all we have that is Christian in our national life and character and also for more of its kind that is still needed."

In 1864, the National Reform Association held a second convention in Allegheny, Pennsylvania, which dispatched a committee of representatives to Washington to meet with President Lincoln and present their Constitutional amendment to Congress. Lincoln dismissed the notion out of hand; Congress sat on it for nine years, before the Judiciary Committee of the House of Representatives affirmed the liberal tradition of America by rejecting it. They responded by saying that this country was founded "to be the home of the oppressed of all nations of the earth, whether Christian or pagan, and in full realization of the dangers which the union between church and state had imposed upon so many nations of the Old World, [our country's founders decided] with great unanimity that it was inexpedient to put anything into the Constitution or frame of government which might be construed to be a reference to any religious creed or doctrine."

Angry leaders of the National Reform Association likened Congressman E. G. Goulet, the chair of the Judiciary Committee, to a "foolhardy fellow who persists in standing on a railroad track . . . when he hears the rumble of the coming train." Espousing a "Christian America, love it or leave it" line, they suggested that if our representatives in Congress "do not see fit to fall in with the majority, they must abide the consequences, or seek some more congenial clime."

> We might add in all justice, if the opponents of the Bible do not like our government and its Christian features, let them go to some wild, desolate land, and in the name of the devil, and for the sake of the devil, subdue it, and set up a government of their own on infidel and atheistic ideas; and then if they can stand it, stay there till they die.

In contrast to the self-appointed protectors of the Bible who banded together in the National Reform Association, Abraham Lincoln honored the spirit of the scriptures, not the letter. Though no more a favorite of the clergy than Thomas Jefferson, Abraham Lincoln founded his political platform on explicitly religious principles. At a time of unprecedented trial, he was our national theologian.

Conscious of our sinful nature, Lincoln judged himself and his country by God's law. Dismissing such groups as the National Reform Association (because their objects were sectarian and counter to the broad faith of our founders), he expressed a larger religious spirit, one consonant with the great liberal tradition he labored to preserve. As he said on his way to the White House in 1861, we are "an almost chosen people."

After visiting the United States, English author and gadfly G. K. Chesterton wrote, "America is the only nation in the world that is founded on a creed. That creed is set forth with dogmatic and even theological lucidity in the Declaration of Independence." Though far from being credal in a dogmatic sense, this creed, or better, covenant, has had few champions more devout than Abraham Lincoln. Throughout his life, Lincoln viewed the Declaration of Independence in a reverential light, describing it as "spiritually regenerative." The touchstone of "our ancient faith," its principles and symbols called forth, "the better angels of our nature." He rarely discussed the slavery issue without hearkening back to Jefferson's words that all of us are created equal, and endowed with certain unalienable rights.

Lincoln's religious beliefs were far from conventional. Raised by Free-will Baptists in Kentucky, the young Lincoln found Thomas Paine's deism more attractive than his parents' Christianity. But as he grew older, suffering through the death of brother, sister, and two sons, and contemplating the carnage of war, Lincoln gradually adopted a liberal Christian outlook.

Even then he held no truck with theologians. "The more a man knew of theology," he once said, "the further he got away from the spirit of Christ." When asked why he refused to join a church, Lincoln replied, "Because I find difficulty without mental reservation in giving my assent to their long and complicated creeds," adding that, "When any church inscribes on its altar, as a qualification for membership, the Savior's statement of the substance of the law and the Gospel—'Thou shalt love the Lord thy God with all thy heart and with all thy soul and with all thy mind . . . and thy neighbor as thyself'—that church will I join with all my heart and soul."

There are as many legendary stories about Lincoln as about Washington, and most make a point that rings true to the spirit of the man. According to one of his first biographers, early in his career, while perusing the voting lists in his home town of Springfield, Lincoln took particular interest in how the local clergy were planning to vote. Of twenty-six clergymen from various denominations, only three had registered as Republicans. According to legend, Lincoln turned to a friend and said, "I am not a Christian—God knows I would be one—but I have carefully read the Bible." He drew a Bible from his pocket, where he always carried it. "These men well know that I am for freedom in the territories, freedom everywhere as far as the Constitution and laws will permit, and that my opponents are for slavery. They know this, and yet, with this book in their hands, in the light of which human bondage cannot live a moment, they are going to vote against me. I do not understand it at all."

> I know there is a God, and that He hates injustice and slavery. I see the storm coming, and I know that His hand is in it. If He has a place and work for me—and I think He has—I believe I am ready. I am nothing, but truth is everything. I know I am right because I know that liberty is right, for Christ teaches it, and Christ is God. I have told them that a house divided against itself cannot stand, and Christ and reason say the same; and they will find it so. Douglas don't care whether slavery is voted up or down, but God cares, and humanity cares, and I care; and with God's help I shall not fail. I may not see the end; but it will come, and I shall be vindicated; and these men will find that they have not read their Bibles aright.

This story may be apocryphal, but it accurately reflects Lincoln's religious views. Once he summed up his faith by repeating something he had heard as a boy: "When I do good, I feel good; when I do bad, I feel bad; and that's my religion." In fact, his religion was more nuanced than that. Combining the prophet Micah's definition of religion ("And what does the Lord require of thee but to do justly, love mercy, and walk humbly with thy God") with the opening words of our Declaration of Independence, he wove together a simple but profound theology, based on the principles of equity, liberty, justice, compassion, and humility.

Lincoln's theology and language were steeped in the books of the Hebrew prophets. Like them, he held himself under the same judgment he pronounced, felt the burden of his special calling, and agonized for himself and his people. Also like them, he felt guided by the spirit. Once, when presented with the possibility of being outvoted, he said, "The probability that we may fall in the struggle ought not to deter us from the support of a cause we believe to be just; it shall not deter me." Lincoln was contemplating something far larger than his own ambition: "If ever I feel the soul within me elevate and expand to those dimensions not wholly unworthy of its Almighty Architect, it is when I contemplate the cause of my country, deserted by all the world beside, and I am standing up boldly and alone and hurling defiance at her victorious oppressors."

For Lincoln the American proposition was a religious proposition. Universal in nature and liberal in spirit, the American covenant transcended all other creeds by placing its adherents under a higher judgment. Answering to this call, Lincoln contributed two major texts to our nation's secular scriptures: the Gettysburg Address and his Second Inaugural Address. Of the latter—to which I shall return—one biographer wrote, "Probably no other speech of a modern statesman uses so unreservedly the language of intense religious feeling."

If less explicitly theological, the Gettysburg Address also is religious both in tone and intent, "a symbolic and sacramental act" according to poet Robert Lowell:

> In his words, Lincoln symbolically died, just as the Union soldiers really died—and as he himself was soon really to die. By his words, he gave the field of battle a symbolic significance that it had lacked. For us and our country, he left Jefferson's ideals of freedom and equality joined to the Christian sacrificial act of death and rebirth. I believe this is a meaning that goes beyond sect or religion and beyond peace and war, and is now part of our lives as a challenge, obstacle and hope.

At the November 19, 1863, dedication of the National Soldiers' Cemetery at Gettysburg, with thousands of soldiers from both sides who gave their lives in early July of that same year being ceremoniously laid to rest, Lincoln's role was a minor one. The sponsors invited him to make "a few appropriate remarks" following the major address to be delivered by Edward Everett of Massachusetts.

Everett, a former U.S. senator, president of Harvard, and Unitarian minister, was the most highly regarded orator of his day. He spoke for two full hours to a crowd of 15,000 on Cemetery Ridge. The Baltimore Glee Club followed by singing a solemn dirge written expressly for the occasion. Only then did Lincoln, his voice clear but unimpassioned, deliver his two-minute address. Upon finishing, he leaned over to Ward Hill Lamon, his military attaché, and said "Lamon, that speech won't scour. It is a flat failure. The people won't like it."

Others agreed, including Secretary of State Seward, who turned to Everett on the platform and said, "He has made a failure and I am sorry for it; his speech is not equal to him." Unlike Everett's address, which often was interrupted by applause, when Lincoln sat down, it was to deafening silence.

A school girl from Spokane, in the audience that day, explained years later that "Applause is out of place at the graves of the dead. It would have been incongruous upon that occasion. Mr. Lincoln's speech was one of consecration, entirely distinct from the rest of the program. Thousands of new made graves surrounded him; the autumn rains had scarcely washed the blood stains from the ground on which we stood. While there were no cheers, there were plenty of tears. They were visible on almost every cheek and there was a silent 'Amen!' in many hearts."

Edward Everett sensed this as well. "Ah, Mr. President," he said, "how gladly would I give my hundred pages to be the author of your twenty lines." The next day he wrote, "I should be glad if I could flatter myself that I came as near to the central idea of the occasion in two hours as you did in two minutes," to which Lincoln replied, "I am pleased to know that, in your judgment, the little I did say was not entirely a failure." In fact, America's liberal covenant has never found more eloquent expression. This brief address cannot be revisited too often.

> Fourscore and seven years ago our fathers brought forth on this continent, a new nation, conceived in liberty, and dedicated to the proposition that all men are created equal.
>
> Now, we are engaged in a great Civil War, testing whether that nation or any nation so conceived and so dedicated can long endure.
>
> We are met on the battlefield of that war, to dedicate a portion of that field as a final resting place to those who here gave their lives that that nation might live. It is altogether fitting and proper that we should do this.
>
> But, in a larger sense, we cannot dedicate—we cannot consecrate—we cannot hallow—this ground. The brave men, living and dead, who struggled here have consecrated it far above our poor power to add or detract. The world will little note nor long remember what we say here, but it can never forget what they did here. It is for us, the living, rather, to be dedicated here to the unfinished work which they who fought here have thus far so nobly advanced.
>
> It is rather for us to be here dedicated to the great task remaining before us—that from these honored dead we take increased devotion to that cause for which they gave the last full measure of devotion; that we here highly resolve that these dead shall not have died in vain; that this nation, under God, shall have a new birth of freedom; and that government of the people, by the people, for the people shall not perish from the earth.

Lincoln's language is biblical in cadence and theme. It is also thoroughly American. This country of, by, and for the people is a nation under God. Through the sacrifices of its citizens and at the time of its greatest trial, our nation, founded on the proposition that all were born equal and invested with certain inalienable rights, could finally attain its moral promise. No wonder Martin Luther King, Jr., echoed Chesterton a century later when he said: "I have a dream that one day this nation will rise up and live out the true meaning of its creed."

Lincoln carefully balanced his faith in liberal democracy with his faith in God. The two reinforced one another. On the eve of the Civil War, in his First Inaugural Address, Lincoln asked, "Why should there not be a patient confidence in the ultimate justice of the people?" Underscoring his belief in the relationship between democratic process and divine will, he added "If the Almighty ruler of nations, with his eternal truth and justice, be on your side of the North or on yours of the South, that truth, and that justice, will surely prevail, by the judgment of this great tribunal, the American people." Unfolding events sobered his optimism, but Lincoln remained convinced that the democratic process, as enshrined in our Constitution, stood best able to approximate God's law, natural and revealed. The promised rebirth of freedom fulfilled our nation's and his savior's commandments. Still, for Abraham Lincoln the question was not whether God was on his side but whether he was on the side of God.

Of course, both parties, abolitionist and slave-holder alike, defended their antithetical positions by marshaling evidence from the Constitution and the scriptures. Even the Declaration of Independence served two masters, with abolitionists interpreting the propositional clause that all are created equal inclusively, and the pro-slavery party responding that the authors' intention clearly excluded people of color.

This divergence lies at the heart of the 1857 Dred Scott Supreme Court decision. A slave who lived for years with his master in Illinois (where slavery had been outlawed in 1787) and Wisconsin (a free state under the provisions of the Missouri Compromise), Scott argued that, having been resident in these states, he was henceforth a free man. The court disagreed.

Rendering the court's opinion, Chief Justice Taney acknowledged the apparent dissonance between the ruling that Negroes could not be considered citizens and Jefferson's pledge to equality in the Declaration of Independence. The justices resolved this discrepancy by claiming that "The legislation and histories of the times, and the language used in the Declaration of Independence, show that neither the class of persons who had been imported as slaves nor their descendants, whether they had become free or not, were then acknowledged as a part of the people nor intended to be included in the general words used in that memorable instrument."

Taney confessed that Jefferson's words might seem to embrace the whole human family, but dismissed this as an illusion, which, if true, would have transformed an otherwise stirring and inspirational document into one that instead would have "deserved and received universal rebuke and reprobation." Since many of our founding fathers themselves held slaves, Taney further argued that to claim that the Declaration of Independence includes people of color among those created equal and vested with certain inalienable rights is to charge its signers with hypocrisy.

The consequences of the Dred Scott decision were staggering. Among other things, now officially not citizens, freed slaves, even in the North, could no longer own property. If not vigorously enforced, as late as 1860 the federal government invoked this interpretation to confiscate land owned by black freedmen. With the preamble of the Declaration of Independence twisted into a defense of slavery, our nation's soul was in jeopardy. Lincoln lamented that the Dred Scott decision rendered "the perfect freedom of the people to be just no freedom at all."

In the famous Lincoln–Douglas debates of 1858, Stephen A. Douglas, who defeated Lincoln for the U.S. Senate in Illinois, defended the Dred Scott decision. He admonished Lincoln, and all other critics of this ruling, pointing out that the Supreme Court has unquestionable authority to interpret the Constitution. Whether we like them or not its decisions should be immune from democratic meddling. Douglas further argued from a states rights position, taken up again during the civil rights debates of the 1950s and 1960s: "I care more for the great principle of self-government, than I do for all the Negroes in Christendom." He then went straight for the emotional jugular at the heart of many people's support of slavery: "I would not blot out the great inalienable rights of the white men for all the Negroes that ever existed. I do not regard the Negro as my equal, and positively deny that he is my brother or any kin to me whatever."

As have many devout people throughout history, Douglas capped his rhetoric by enlisting God as a witness for his ungodly cause.

> I do not believe that the Almighty ever intended the Negro to be the equal of the white man. If he did, he has been a long time demonstrating the fact. For thousands of years the Negro has been a race upon the earth, and during all that time, in all latitudes and climates, wherever he has wandered or been taken, he has been inferior to the race which he has there met. He belongs to an inferior race and must always occupy an inferior position.

Lincoln could have quoted from Isaiah 4 ("He will make justice shine on every race"). But, perceiving the intimate relationship between liberal democracy and the ideals of equity and justice, he instead chose to cite chapter and verse of the American covenant:

> According to our ancient faith, the just powers of governments are derived from the consent of the governed. Now the relation of master and slave is *pro tanto* [to that extent] a total violation of this principle. The master not only governs the slave without his consent but he governs him by a set of rules altogether different from those which he prescribes for himself. Allow all the governed an equal voice in the government, and that, and that only, is self-government.

Charging Douglas with "blowing out the moral lights around us," and with "penetrating the human soul and eradicating the light of reason and the love of liberty in this American people," in a voice thinner but morally far more resonant than that of his eloquent opponent, Lincoln reclaimed the

Declaration of Independence from its recent captivity. "A house divided against itself cannot stand," he said, quoting from the Bible. "I believe this government cannot endure, permanently, half slave and half free."

Lincoln was seeking a "more perfect union," one built on the vision of Washington, Jefferson, and Madison. Pointing out their acquiescence to slavery, Judge Taney and Stephen Douglas read intention into our founding fathers' actions and thus rationalized perpetuation of the status quo. But Lincoln had an answer for this as well. In 1794, a Congress composed of our nation's founders banned taking slaves out of the United States to sell; in 1798, they prohibited slave trafficking in the Mississippi Territory; in 1803, they restrained internal slave trade; in 1808, they imposed heavy financial and corporal penalties against African slave traders; and in 1820, they declared the slave trade to be piracy, and thus punishable by death.

In today's court, on questions ranging from gun control to minority rights, constitutional experts continue to weigh the "intent" of its framers in the balance of their words. Even as theologians get trapped by ancient prejudices contained in the scriptures, a strict constitutional constructionist can easily fall prey to prejudices common to the eighteenth century, even among liberals. Far from simply constituting a ninth-grade civics lesson, revisiting the debate over slavery should prompt our vigilance toward anyone who employs either the scriptures or the Constitution to defend an illiberal value system.

What contemporary politician or jurist champions slavery on the grounds that certain framers of our constitution owned slaves? And what theologian or preacher would wish to reinstitute it on the grounds that slavery is sanctioned here and there in the Bible? Yet, throughout the mid-nineteenth century, pro-slavery advocates peppered their rhetoric with biblical quotations. "Slavery was ordained by God," they said. "It was imposed as a curse upon the descendants of Ham. And Paul wrote that slaves should obey their masters. Read your Bible," they said. "Slavery is Christian. And those who oppose it are not."

Whenever people cite the biblical letter in defiance of its spirit, that's the way the logic twists. This continues today, when fundamentalists marshal chapter and verse as proof-texts in their campaigns against homosexual, women's, or minority rights. How does this differ from their predecessors' employment of the scriptures to defend slavery?

Ralph Waldo Emerson made the same point when condemning the Fugitive Slave Law. His eloquent argument should haunt anyone who rifles the scriptures for ammunition in defense of neighborly hate:

> One would have said that a Christian would not keep slaves; but the Christians keep slaves. Of course they will not dare to read the Bible. Won't they? They quote the Bible, quote Paul, quote Christ to justify slavery. If slavery is good, then is lying, theft, arson, homicide, each and all good, and to be maintained by Union societies.
>
> These things show that no forms, neither constitutions, nor laws, nor covenants, nor churches, nor Bibles, are of any use in themselves. The devil nestles comfortably into them all. There is no help but in the head and heart and hamstrings of a man. . . . To interpret Christ it needs Christ in the heart. The teachings of the Spirit can be apprehended only by the same spirit that gave them forth.

Christ's emblem in the heart is love, to God and one's neighbor. The teachings of the Spirit are those of the prophets, who proclaimed, as inscribed on the Liberty Bell, "liberty throughout the land to all the inhabitants thereof." Christ and the prophets—love and justice—together inspired Abraham Lincoln's political theology.

One reason the prophetic role is crucial to the liberal tradition is that without it we could easily rest on the rhetoric of our ideals, without realizing how far we are from putting them into practice. Prophets shame us into recognizing that any offer of selective liberty is a prescription for injustice.

I think of prophet Sojourner Truth, who, in 1851, when

challenged as a woman for speaking up in church, shouted out, "He say women can't have as much rights as men, 'cause Christ wan't a woman! . . . Whar did your Christ come from? From God and a woman! Man had nothin' to do wid Him."

I think of Frederick Douglass, who, forced on account of his color to ride in the baggage car when traveling by train through Pennsylvania, replied to one passenger who tried to comfort him: "They cannot degrade Frederick Douglass. The soul that is within me no man can degrade. I am not the one that is being degraded on account of this treatment, but those who are inflicting it upon me."

I think of Susan B. Anthony, who insisted on casting a vote for president in 1872, at a time when suffrage was denied to "idiots, criminals, lunatics, and women."

I think of her soul mate, Elizabeth Cady Stanton, who called for a new kind of woman: "brave, courageous, self-reliant, . . . [women] who in the face of adverse winds have kept one steady course upward and onward in the paths of virtue and peace; they who have taken their gauge of womanhood from their own native strength and dignity; they who have learned for themselves the will of God concerning them."

The century-long campaigns for civil rights and women's rights challenge liberal democracy to live up to its promise: liberty to each and justice for all. They call us home to the spirit of the scriptures and the faith of our nation's founders: the self-evident truth that all people are created equal; a government of, by and for the people; the love of God and our neighbor as ourself.

Nowhere is this more evident than in Lincoln's Second Inaugural Address, delivered only months before he died. He fulfills the prophet's ancient role: to speak the word of God without hubris. Considering it "perhaps better than anything I have produced," he did acknowledge that it would not be immediately popular. "Men are not flattered by being shown that there has been a difference of purpose between the Almighty and them."

In an eight-minute speech, the shortest inaugural address on record, Lincoln begins by acknowledging that during the late conflict between North and South both sides read the same Bible and petitioned the same God for assistance against the other. "It may seem strange that any men should dare to ask a just God's assistance in wringing their bread from the sweat of other men's faces," Lincoln said, "but let us judge not that we be not judged." In God's good time, justice would ultimately be done and the ungodly institution of slavery abolished. Even then, however, given our sinful nature, the prayers of neither side would be answered fully. Our judgments are themselves under a higher judgment, one we cannot presume perfectly to discern, whereas "The judgments of the Lord are true and righteous altogether."

In closing, Lincoln expresses the essence of the liberal gospel. The key to following in the spirit of the scriptures is to practice neighborly love:

> With malice toward none, with charity for all, with firmness in the right as God gives us to see the right, let us strive on to finish the work we are in, to bind up the nation's wounds, to care for him who shall have borne the battle and for his widow and his orphan—to do all which may achieve and cherish a just and lasting peace among ourselves and with all nations.

During Abraham Lincoln's tenure, Congress passed a law mandating that the words "In God We Trust" be placed on all our currency. Contrast this with the secular motto, "Mind your business," which was proposed for our money by Benjamin Franklin. "Mind your business" does have a certain hard-headed, no-nonsense all-American appeal. But it fails to acknowledge any power beyond our own. Sectarian expressions of religion may be toxic to liberal democracy, but the lowest common denominator of secularism is almost equally deleterious, as it tends to displace moral values by giving false ultimacy to the values of the marketplace.

Avoiding both the rocks of sectarianism and the shoals of

secularism, in the great American liberal tradition Abraham Lincoln devoted, even gave his life, to preserve "one nation under God." Enjoining neighborliness and justice—or liberty with equity—"even to the least of these," Abraham Lincoln held Christ in his heart, and followed in the spirit of the prophets. In the words of Isaiah, "Ours were the suffering he bore, ours the sorrows he carried. . . . He was pierced through for our faults, crushed for our sins. On him lies a punishment that brings us peace, and through his wounds we are healed."

Revisiting our nation's history pays dividends. We need to reacquaint ourselves with the architects and prophets who established and protected our ideals. Such pilgrimages are important, as Lincoln reminds us in his First Inaugural Address. Through them "The mystic chords of memory, stretching from every battlefield and patriot grave to every living heart and hearthstone all over this broad land, will yet swell the chorus of the Union, when again touched, as surely they will be, by the better angels of our nature."

These better angels are liberal angels, angels of mercy, angels of liberty and justice for all.

# III

# *Reclaiming the Family*

# 7

# *Your Mother Is a Liberal*

> In the different voice of women lies the truth of an ethic of care, the tie between relationship and responsibility, and the origins of aggression in the failure of connection.
>
> —Carol Gilligan

If, as our pilgrimage through American history suggests, the spirit of the scriptures and our nation's founders and prophets is profoundly liberal, how can one explain the eclipse of liberalism over the past quarter century. One reason is this: The word *liberal* became synonymous with big government, especially government welfare and social assistance programs. Though Roosevelt's New Deal won the approval of most American citizens, and Lyndon Johnson's Great Society nearly as many, by the bicentennial year a new consensus was forming. In 1980, Ronald Reagan was swept into office (and a dozen Democratic U.S. senators including my father swept out) on a tide of antiliberal, antigovernment sentiment. The airwaves were jammed with rhetoric excoriating "tax-and-spend" liberals, liberal "giveaway programs," "fuzzy-headed" liberals; the L word turned out to be by far the most effective hook on which to hang an opponent.

Consequently, by 1982 the number of congressional and senatorial candidates who openly owned the liberal label could probably be counted on two hands. One by one, the domestic programs initiated by President Johnson were cut back, victims of antigovernment fervor. And during each of the past twelve years the gap between rich and poor in this country has grown.

Even were it possible, which it is not, a return to the impersonal aspects of big-government liberalism would be ill-advised. There may be many selfish reasons for the popular backlash against the Great Society programs, but one good reason is that the federal government is an inefficient and ineffective provider of direct social services in areas such as public housing. Here bigger is not better, simply more cumbersome, fraught with red tape and bureaucratic bumbling. On the other hand, our national retreat from a commitment to social justice and equity has taken a terrible toll on the American spirit, and carries hidden costs that far outweigh the short-term savings. Until the public spirit of compassion and neighborliness revives, this corrosive pattern will continue, and not only the poor but eventually everyone will suffer.

By definition, the liberal spirit is adaptive to changing social and political realities. This is not a weakness. An open mind is not necessarily an empty mind; it is a mind capable of forming new opinions in response to new information. For instance, in earlier centuries, when bondage, whether religious or political, shackled the liberty of the human mind, the liberal voice proclaimed a gospel of individual freedom—freedom of thought, freedom of speech, freedom of belief. That was right and good. But times have changed.

In our country today the besetting crisis is not one of bondage but of bondlessness. The societal fabric is ripping apart. To preserve the greatest good for the greatest number, we must find ways to bond together in redemptive community. The past decades teach us that community cannot be instilled by government programs alone, however well intentioned their architects. On the other hand, given the growing inequities in society, for millions of our citizens a pull-yourself-up-by-your-own-bootstrap ethic is both cruel and dysfunctional. Together we must find a better way.

To nurture the spirit of community, liberals might begin by

reclaiming a third symbol in addition to Bible and flag: the family. It won't be easy. As "pro-family" advocates the religious and political right have established an almost exclusive rhetorical franchise. Yet a true pro-family policy, not based on moralistic strictures, but one that takes into account all of our children, can only be shaped by the liberal spirit.

Motherhood is the most poignant rhetorical emblem of the family, so before turning to the larger issues of community building, I shall begin with mothers, including my own. Regardless of her politics, I believe that any good mother is by nature a liberal, and therefore deserves to be listed among the greatest liberals of all time.

Of course, one goal of many so-called "pro-family" advocates is to protect mothers from liberals: to protect them from being raped by criminals on furlough; to protect them from losing their children to the seductions of rock lyrics, secular humanist literature, and permissive sex. Such rhetoric is effective, and for good reason. With the possible exception of God, no symbol, including flag and Bible, packs more emotional wallop than the word *mother.*

Not that conservatives are the only ones whose sentimental heart strings are easily plucked. I was certainly moved, when, after a particularly brilliant performance, I once saw tears in a 250-pound linebacker's eyes as he confessed to a national television audience that he owed everything to his mother.

He was probably right. Abandoned by his father at an early age, it was his mother who raised him and his brothers and sisters. She nurtured him and sacrificed for him, taught him the difference between right and wrong, was always there for him.

He may be numbered among the fortunate ones. Lacking a national family policy, with proper childcare, education, and job training programs, many of his friends fell through the cracks. They are not dead or in jail or working the drug lanes because of liberal permissiveness. On the contrary. Lured by the sirens of Madison Avenue, filling the airwaves with dream visions of fast cars, slick shoes, and hot women, they chased the American dream into the only alley available to them. Once trapped there, even their mothers couldn't save them.

If you want to protect a mother, you must first protect her children. One famous American liberal, Julia Ward Howe, reminded us of this more than a century ago.

In 1870, five years after the cessation of hostilities between North and South, the Franco-Prussian War broke out in Europe. A senseless conflict, it galvanized the small but growing band of international peace activists. Director of the Perkins School for the Blind in Boston, founder of the first American women ministers group, popular poet, and author of "The Battle Hymn of the Republic," Howe, who as an abolitionist had strongly supported the Union cause, now figured prominently among the American crusaders for peace.

She wrote a manifesto against the Franco-Prussian War, had it translated into five languages (French, German, Italian, Spanish, and Swedish), and then set out for Europe intending to deliver it at international peace conferences in London and Paris. But because she was a woman, the European organizers denied her a place on the program. Angry but undaunted, she hired her own hall, and posted broadsides inviting the public to hear her. Few people came. So she returned to the United States, not broken but inspired with a new idea. She called it Mother's Day.

In Howe's original conception, Mother's Day was designed to draw attention to several basic liberal values. Her object was not to put mothers on a pedestal. She wanted to draw mothers out of their kitchens and parlors into the public square, to unite as many women as she could in a common cause: the protection of children from war. Or, as she put it, "to promote the alliance of the different nationalities, the amicable settlement of international questions, the great and general interests of peace." Significantly, she didn't call her annual festival International Peace Day; she called it Mother's Day, knowing no group that could more naturally or persuasively sponsor an annual festival of love and peace.

On June 2, 1870, Howe issued the first Mother's Day proclamation. She called upon "all women who have hearts, whether your baptism be that of water or of tears," to say firmly:

> We will not have great questions decided by irrelevant agencies. Our husbands shall not come to us, reeking with carnage, for caresses and applause. Our sons shall not be taken from us to unlearn all that we have been able to teach them of charity, mercy and patience. We women of one country will be too tender of those of another country to allow our sons to be trained to injure theirs. From the bosom of the devastated earth a voice goes up with our own. It says "Disarm, Disarm! The sword of murder is not the balance of justice."

Linking motherhood, mother earth, womanhood, and peace, Howe asserted that the unconditional love they hold for their children invests mothers with a natural and deep interest in preventing bloodshed. Fathers send their sons to war; mothers remain at home to grieve. Who could better symbolize the need for peace than any soldier's mother? Mother's Day would remind everyone that the whole world would be a better place, if only everyone might rise to the challenge of motherhood: nurturing life, fostering peace, giving love. "Let women now leave all that may be left of home for a great and earnest day of counsel," she proclaimed. "Let them meet first, as women, to bewail and commemorate the dead. Let them then solemnly take counsel with each other as to the means whereby the great human family can live in peace, each bearing after his own time the sacred impress, not of Caesar, but of God."

For several years, on June 2 in New York, Boston, and Philadelphia—also in England, Scotland, and Switzerland—Mother's Day was celebrated in this spirit. As with many of our national festivals, more recently it has fallen on hard times. What began as a celebration of the second great commandment (to love thy neighbor as thyself) has devolved into a commercial holiday cosponsored by the florist and card industries.

Rather than calling on mothers to unite, rally, march, and proclaim to the world the values they so liberally bestow on their children, we celebrate their domesticity with flowers and cliché rhymes.

Julia Ward Howe had it right. What good mothers have in common is not that they stay at home with the children. Far more importantly, they instill in those same children a respect for others, generosity of spirit, cooperation, forgiveness, and loving kindness—fundamental liberal values. This is no less true of nurturing fathers. But since (along with the Bible and flag) not fatherhood but motherhood has been co-opted as a right-wing "pro-family" trademark, it is important to remind ourselves that good mothers, regardless of their politics, are liberal by nature.

I can't speak about mothers in general without saying a few words about my own. If all good mothers are generic liberals, my mother takes the cake. She slips easily into almost every adjective that adorns the term: open-hearted, open-minded, open-handed. Not to mention permissive and profligate.

Her name is Bethine—be thine—and that's the way she's lived her life, for others. But also for herself. As those women know who have given themselves away without return, to love your neighbor as yourself is a cruel adage if you don't love and respect yourself. Yet, as with many women, any superficial description of my mother makes her sound like someone else's property. The daughter of a governor, Chase Clark. The wife of a U.S. senator. This is misleading.

Actually she's the best politician in the family, knowing better than any of us that "politics is people." She certainly would have understood and rallied to Julia Ward Howe's vision of Mother's Day.

Alluding to their liberal politics, my mother recalled that "At one time in Idaho, I remember three Clarks on the same ticket—my father for Mayor of our town, my uncle for Governor, and my cousin for the U.S. Senate. The opposition got out a yellow sheet entitled 'Clark, Clark, Clark, said the little red hen.' "

My usually mild-tempered grandmother was livid. She said to her husband, "Chase, do you know who put this out? It's full of lies."

"Yes," he replied, "but that's just fine. We didn't have a chance before, but this will elect all three of us." He was right. How times have changed.

As a mother, she was more than liberal. Even Dr. Spock proved insufficiently permissive. To my great delight, from first grade on we conspired to see how many creative excuses we could come up with to keep me home from school. My mother was what these days we call a codependent. I came home one year with three Cs and three Ds; she blamed my teacher.

She even saved me from the bomb. It was 1958. Fire drills in elementary school had been temporarily replaced by nuclear attack drills. The alarm would go off and all of us would dutifully tuck ourselves under our desks. From the moment of the first alert to the arrival of the missiles, we had ten minutes. Three times a year we practiced this. I can assure you (and some of you will remember), ten minutes pass very slowly when you are crouching under your desk waiting for an imaginary nuclear bomb to fall.

So I planned my escape, and practiced by running home after school every day. Despite an innate lack of athletic ability, I finally got it down under ten minutes. One day I arrived panting at the door, and my mother, fearing that once again I had attracted the attention of neighborhood bullies, asked me why I was so winded. I told her of my plan. She understood completely. "If there ever were a nuclear attack, I'd want you here with me, not at school under your stupid desk."

So my mother went to the principal and requested that, in the event of nuclear attack, I might have permission to run home and die with her. The result was a new school policy. Should a nuclear attack take place, upon securing parental permission those children who could get home within ten minutes would be excused from school.

Each of us learns different things from his or her parents,

but there are ways in which all nurturing parents are alike. Through the unconditional gift of their love and the security offered by sheltering arms and the comfort of home, we learn to trust others and life itself. More by example than instruction, our parents also teach us how to balance freedom and responsibility, individual wants and community needs. Both are first modeled in the family, with its one body and several members.

Like the church, at one level, the family is a conservative institution. It establishes boundaries, maintains tradition, and performs a stabilizing role in society. Each of these functions is noble, and the breakdown of the family is surely a distressing symptom, perhaps even direct cause, of the breakdown of societal values.

On the other hand, within the family the maternal role (whether performed by a mother, father, grandparent, or older sibling) is one of modeling and inculcating liberal values: hospitality, neighborliness, forgiveness, compassion, tender loving care. Liberals do not possess these traits any more surely than do conservatives, or even Marxists for that matter. Anyone can be a bad parent, regardless of his or her politics or religion. Maternal values may be considered liberal only to the same extent that such offerings of the heart as generosity and charitability bespeak a liberal temperament.

Maternal gifts are not proffered in exchange for good behavior. As with all tokens of liberality, they are given freely without demand for an equivalent return. Nurturing mothers do not dole out love on a point system. The prodigal child may even receive more than the dutiful one. Good mothers give their children what they deserve only in the broadest sense of the term, that of natural entitlement. Every child deserves parental love, not because of what he or she does but because of who he or she is—a part of the human family, a child of God.

Though it extends even beyond childhood, and is poignantly demonstrated when children come of age and parents set them free to find their own way in the world, the liberal nature of parenthood is perhaps most evident in the interplay between mothers and infants. Tiny babies do nothing to earn our love. Perceiving the world about them—especially their mothers—as mere extensions of their own being, they have only a selfish interest at heart. Endlessly demanding, driven instinctively by biological needs, infants therefore require liberal ministrations of maternal care. Good mothers give this freely, generously, bounteously. They offer milk and warmth, hugs and caresses, all of which the child initially takes for granted, without offering even a smile in return.

When my son was born this hit me with the force of revelation: how much my own parents had worried about and fussed over me, fed and rocked and suckled me, without my being conscious of anything save my own appetites. Parents reap unquestionable rewards, but the balance of giving and receiving can only be struck by lavishing on our own children the love and concern that our parents bestowed on us.

One reason family values are rarely associated with liberalism is that the religious and political right possess undeniable skill in manipulating symbols. After years of impassioned repetition, the term *pro-family* (together with pro-life, Bible-believing, and pro-American) has come to represent the antithesis of liberal, which by extension becomes *antifamily* (antilife, Bible-despising, and anti-American). Rather than uniting us as a people—the vast majority of whom share, regardless of faith or politics, a profound respect for Bible, flag, and family—our most powerful symbols are being rhetorically exploited for narrow, sectarian, divisive, and sometimes even bigoted ends.

Much pro-family rhetoric has little to do with the family. Antiabortion advocates insist that every pregnancy come to term, which would indeed increase the number of children. Then many of them turn around and campaign against prenatal care and childcare bills, more federal aid to education, and other social welfare measures that would enhance those same children's lives, given that so many of those affected are numbered among the poorest of our neighbors.

Other "family" issues include campaigns against pornography and in favor of prayer in the public schools. Neither issue concerns the family as directly as do education and healthcare. And both campaigns propose cures that would be costly to our heritage of freedom. Yet, when civil libertarians cite the First Amendment to remind us that our nation was founded on the great principles of freedom of speech and freedom of religion, they are often branded as child-defiling smut-purveyors and atheists.

Even as it is difficult to win a fistfight with a bully, the so-called pro-family moral lobby holds a tremendous rhetorical advantage over those who fear the abridgment of constitutional rights more than the latitude such rights offer for possible abuse. This is ironic. Until recently there was no pornography behind the Iron Curtain. Now it is an entrepreneurial growth industry. In China, where the communist line is holding, the penalty for selling pornography is death. I doubt that anyone would argue that the purchase of freedom is not worth the price of pornography. Yet, as the barriers to free expression fall in Eastern Europe, in the United States we are toying with the idea of thought police.

School libraries are being censored. Among the books ordered from the shelves are *The Diary of Anne Frank* and *The Wizard of Oz*. The National Endowment for the Arts is struggling for its very existence, threatened by congressional critics whose artistic credentials are far less conspicuous than their gift for manipulating constituent fears in order to get re-elected. Given the problems we face, and all the real family issues that go begging, the true obscenity is that a battle against funding "obscene" art could become the centerpiece of a senatorial campaign, or that educational reformers obsess more on what children should not read than on improving education by providing the monies necessary to enhance teacher training and attract better teachers through higher pay.

I have no truck with pornography. Few liberals do. And I have no problem with local ordinances imposing restrictions on it. The utilization of children in kiddie-porn is grotesque and rightly banned. There is no reason why pornographic magazines should not be wrapped in plastic covers to prevent children from perusing them. And, in terms of government funding for the arts, if certain projects are deemed pornographic or obscene, there is also no reason why the government must be commandered as a cash cow for freedom of expression. Here the separation of church and state offers a reasonable model, protecting both artists and citizens.

But we mustn't lose sight of priorities. Children are being violated today less by sexually explicit rock lyrics than they are by shoddy schools, poor diets, and endemic poverty. The majority of those who live below the poverty level in this country are children. We have one of the highest infant mortality rates in the western world. Anyone who is truly pro-family will put these issues, not pornography or school prayer, at the top of our social agenda.

Another reason that liberals tend to be more pro-family than illiberal moralists is that we define the family descriptively rather than prescriptively. In today's America a significant minority of people living together in family groupings reflect the 1950s storybook model of Mom, Dad, Dick, Jane, Spot, and Puff. Any pro-family policy that excludes divorced families, single-parent households, those headed by grandmothers with a missing generation in between, unmarried couples with or without children, and the various configurations of extended families often gathered out of economic necessity ignores the needs of the vast majority of American families and most of America's children.

To meet the wide variety of human needs represented by the contemporary American family requires great generosity of spirit. How can a judgmental, moralistic policy, one lacking provisions to relieve special burdens, such as those suffered by single mothers with children, qualify as pro-family?

In a pluralistic society, it is impossible to establish security by imposing standards of uniformity. If our security lies in cultivating strong families, every family is involved, not only those that fit a sentimental stereotype. Our goal should be to cultivate an ethic based on maternal values such as self-giving, generosity, compassion, and tenderness. As we discover the nature of our interdependencies—that when one suffers we all suffer, that we and our neighbor, even we and our enemy, are truly kin—a new family policy emerges, one that avoids moralistic rhetoric, honors differences, and meets existing needs.

The United States and South Africa are the only two major countries without an active government policy to nurture and protect families. "Pro-family" conservatives who prefer tax cuts to government intervention may have a keen eye for the moral breakdown in society, but that is no substitute for a family policy. No combination of judgmental rhetoric and pious exhortation will come close to addressing the systemic collapse of the American family.

Furthermore, it's bad economics: Projections show that every dollar saved in our refusal to bail out the family ultimately costs us several more. As economist Sylvia Ann Hewlett points out in her new book, *When the Bough Breaks: The Cost of Neglecting Our Children*, "What we have done to our children has leashed an avalanche of alienation and violence that is compromising the quality of all of our lives; what is happening to our children is undermining the competitive strength of our nation and threatening the standard of living of all Americans. . . . The human and economic costs of neglecting our children have, quite simply, reached intolerable levels."

The statistics she marshals are staggering. One-quarter of all preschool children live below the poverty level, a figure more than twice than of adult Americans. More than a quarter of all children fail to graduate from high school. We have an estimated one million homeless families.

Apart from the human factor, neglected children become problem children at an extraordinary cost to society. One estimate puts it at $300,000 per child. Every dollar spent on prenatal care saves more than $3 in hospitalization costs for premature babies. In 1990, the White House Task Force on Infant Mortality estimated that one-quarter of the 40,000 infant deaths that occur yearly in this country could easily be prevented, as could many of the 100,000 handicaps that may accompany premature births. Recommending an expansion of

Medicaid coverage and additional doctor incentives to ensure that Medicaid patients will receive good care, the Task Force calls for a half-billion-dollar increase in government funding for prenatal care. That may seem like a lot of money until one considers that, over a lifetime, a low-birth-weight baby may incur medical expenses of some $400,000.

This is just one small part of our missing family policy. Lacking preschool programs and then falling through the cracks of the education system, uneducated children fail to possess the skills necessary to power an information-driven economy. Poverty-stricken children may grow up alcoholic and drug-ridden, taxing the medical delivery system, and thereby bleeding the public purse. Many also become wards of our state penitentiary system, each one costing upward of $20,000 per year. In the last thirty years, New York City's murder rate is up sixfold, and 60 percent of all murders are committed by people twenty-five or under.

As for those who think the answer to crime is capital punishment, most of the punishment delivered by this cure is inflicted on society. It costs $602,000 to incarcerate a person for forty years. From $1.8 to $7 million is required to prosecute each capital case. Creating a vicious circle, each new generation of children is further victimized, for many of the dollars spent on new jails and additional policemen are picked directly from its teachers' pockets.

We need nothing less than a Marshall plan to save our children. A liberal pro-family policy would dispense with moral posturing and self-righteous rhetoric, replacing both with vigorous remedial action to address this crisis at its source. Education must become our first priority, with strong emphasis on preschool programs, better paid and trained teachers, more exciting schools, a longer school year, enhanced educational programming, and more adequate educational loan and job training programs. Though expensive, anything we do to save our children will be cost-effective in the long run. "If you take good care of children they will add to the productive capability of an economy; if you fail to look after children, they will drag a nation down," Hewlett writes. "The critical business of building strong families can no longer be defined as a private endeavor."

Given the dimensions of the crisis, our government will have to play a central role not only in education but also in providing drug treatment on demand, strong federal restrictions on firearms, income tax credits, and a higher minimum wage to raise working families above the poverty level. Each is critical to any comprehensive family policy.

But as we have learned from certain excesses (not of heart but ambition) during the Great Society years, the government alone cannot save our children any more than it could abolish poverty. Acting out of enlightened self-interest, corporations will have to play their part, offering liberal parental leave programs, childcare in the workplace, job-sharing opportunities, and more latitude for those who wish to use home as a workplace. Corporations and their employees can also take a far more active role in fostering good education, both through direct involvement in the public schools and through various corporate sponsorship programs, such as guaranteed scholarships or jobs for high-school graduates.

Religion has an important role to play as well. The church I serve offers a case study for how religion can do its part. Four years ago, Sylvia Ann Hewlett's pioneering work (Sylvia and her family are active members of All Souls) prompted us to establish a Children's Task Force. We focused our initial efforts at New York's Prince George Welfare Hotel, where 1,100 homeless children were warehoused with their families. Out of this grew four church-sponsored scout troops. In a society where gold chains are status symbols and the main forms of social organization are pimp or drug families and wilding packs, some 80 children were given uniforms, nature outings and survival training, summer camp, lots of gold and silver pins and merit badges, and most important of all, adult mentors—big brothers and sisters who guide and nurture them.

The Prince George has closed its doors, its 400 families

scattered throughout the boroughs, but our scout troops continue to thrive in East Harlem. Inspired by this success, in concert with the Franklin and Eleanor Roosevelt Institute, we adopted a public school. Members of the church assist in coaching and tutorial work; offer summer camp scholarships, computers, and copy machines; build and organize the library; work as teachers' assistants; and sponsor an afterschool theater workshop that has fifty enrollees. There is no conflict between church and school. In the liberal tradition, our object is not to save souls but to serve them.

Expanding this mission, All Souls has struck up a sister-church relationship with the Church of the Resurrection in East Harlem. Many of the children cared for there stem from broken, crack-infested families. Several are being raised by their grandmothers. Every day after school, Pastor Leroy Ricksy and All Souls members do two hours of one-on-one tutorial work with fifty children. After just one year, the results are measurable. Third-graders who couldn't read, write, or add, well on their way to becoming statistics (dropouts, junkies, murderers), now go to school not to hide or misbehave but to develop their newfound skills. They too have mentors, who love and teach and care for them as their parents could not.

In a way, these are our children. We provide the tenderness, security, instruction, and guidance they crave and so desperately need. In accordance with the maternal virtues, a liberal surrogate parent offers not moralistic strictures but generous helpings of unconditional, if often very tough, love. Such love is a self-renewing resource. Quoting St. Paul, Sylvia Ann Hewlett explains why so many All Souls parishioners have involved themselves in our Children's Task Force: "Beyond some level of accomplishment, earning power and self-realization become poor substitutes for the higher values of compassion, communion, and charity towards others. 'Though I speak with the tongues of men and angels and have not charity I am becoming as a sounding brass or a tinkling cymbal . . . I am nothing.' "

My mother taught me this. Together with my father, she also taught me that citizenship in a free country is a responsibility, not a luxury. It is an old-fashioned idea, the one upon which our nation was founded.

And she taught me that all of us are related; we are kin to one another in a single human family. She learned this liberal principle—the principle of neighborliness—from her grandmother, whom she once called "the most ecumenical person I ever met." Speaking at the Martin Luther King, Jr., celebration last year in Boise, Idaho, my mother told a story about her grandmother to illustrate two things: Though we are each different, in essence we are one; and, because we are different, we have a hard time understanding one another sometimes.

"My grandmother Clark was very upright and moral. Her favorite poem was 'No sex in heaven.' This title caused some confusion for me until I was old enough to read and understand that the word was spelled s-e-c-t-s.

"In this poem, everyone went down to the River Jordan, and on the trip to the other side, all their robes and vestments were washed away. This, too, confused me—that she could approve and be so pleased about all these grown-ups walking out of the water in their birthday suits. The memory reminds me of how easily we can misunderstand things even with everything clear before us."

My mother spoke that day of Abraham Lincoln and the Emancipation Proclamation. She spoke of the bravery it took to march up to the schoolhouse door in Little Rock, to march for integration in the South, to defy the bans against free assembly in South Africa.

Julia Ward Howe would have been proud, proud to hear my mother give public expression to the maternal ethic of care and tenderness. She would also have understood her choice of holidays in which to proclaim these liberal values. Today, the Martin Luther King, Jr., holiday is a far more appropriate occasion for their expression than is Mother's Day itself.

In 1913, when Congress moved the date from June 2 to the second Sunday in May, it also changed the significance of

Mother's Day. What had been a festival in which mothers might witness publicly to maternal values has been reduced to a private holiday on which their husbands send them cards and roses.

Like Julia Ward Howe, my mother has it right. Motherhood has nothing to do with pedestals, and everything to do with love, justice, and peace. As Bethine Church said in her closing words about Martin Luther King, Jr.: "Let us here today and in our daily lives all be prepared to love and care about each other, to let our differences strengthen rather than diminish us. Let us give up fear of each other and change it into belief in ourselves and our ability to add healing in this often injured world."

The liberal gospel: spoken like a true mother.

# 8

# *E Pluribus Unum*

Since the beginning of our American history, we have been engaged in change—in a perpetual peaceful revolution—a revolution which goes on steadily, quietly adjusting itself to changing conditions. . . . The world order which *we* seek is the cooperation of free countries, working together in a friendly, civilized society.

—FRANKLIN DELANO ROOSEVELT

FROM STORIES THAT MY parents and grandparents told me, Franklin Roosevelt, by far the most famous and influential liberal of our century, became my boyhood hero. Anyone seeking a manifesto for a new liberal agenda need look no further than his presidential papers, specifically in the peroration of his address to Congress on January 6, 1941.

> There is nothing mysterious about the foundations of a healthy and strong democracy. The basic things expected by our people of their political and economic systems are simple. They are:
>
> Equality of opportunity for youth and for others.
>
> Jobs for those who can work.
>
> Security for those who need it.
>
> The ending of special privilege for the few.

> The preservation of civil liberties for all.
>
> The enjoyment of the fruits of scientific progress in a wider and constantly rising standard of living.
>
> These are the simple [and] basic things that must never be lost sight of in the turmoil and unbelievable complexity of our modern world. The inner and abiding strength of our economic and political systems is dependent upon the degree to which they fulfill these expectations.

Fifty years later only his final point rings hollow. The march of material progress brought with it an orgy of consumption and pollution. Over the long term this jeopardizes the commonweal, especially so long as American consumer values capture the imagination of people around the globe. Each of the other aspirations, however, remains central to any restatement of liberal goals in a rapidly changing world.

The most memorable part of Roosevelt's speech was added at the last moment, in his seventh draft. It is a global vision based on the attainment of four essential freedoms.

> The first is freedom of speech and expression—everywhere in the world.
>
> The second is freedom of every person to worship God in his own way—everywhere in the world.
>
> The third is freedom from want—which, translated into world terms, means economic understandings which will secure to every nation a healthy peacetime life for its inhabitants—everywhere in the world.
>
> The fourth is freedom from fear—which, translated into world terms, means a world-wide reduction of armaments to such a point and in such a thorough fashion that no nation will be in a position to commit an act of physical aggression against any neighbor—anywhere in the world. . . .
>
> This nation has placed its destiny in the hands and heads and hearts of its millions of free men and women; and its

> faith in freedom under the guidance of God. Freedom means the supremacy of human rights everywhere. Our support goes to those who struggle to gain those rights and keep them. Our strength is in our unity of purpose.

When Roosevelt finished dictating this passage, he invited comments from the staff members present in the Oval Office. Harry Hopkins, one of the president's principal advisors, questioned the phrase "everywhere in the world."

"That covers an awful lot of territory, Mr. President," he said. "I don't know how interested Americans are going to be in the people of Java."

Roosevelt's reply proved prescient. "I'm afraid they'll have to be some day, Harry. The world is getting so small that even the people in Java are getting to be our neighbors now."

The file of clippings that Roosevelt consulted as he was writing this speech contains two sources for his lists of six foundations and four freedoms. The first is a quote from an "economic bill of rights" circulating in England, setting international minimum standards for housing, food, education, and medical care, along with free speech, free press, and free worship. The second is a list of five proposals offered in an unprecedented joint statement by Catholic and Protestant leaders in England.

1. That extreme inequalities of wealth be abolished
2. Full education for all children, regardless of class or race
3. Protection for the family
4. Restoration of a sense of divine vocation to daily work
5. Use of all the resources of the earth for the benefit of the whole human race

In such statements as these we see the beginning of a liberal global consciousness, one balancing individual rights with community values. Though New Deal liberalism is often viewed as the beginning of state or big-government liberalism, its spirit lies here, in a recognition of the interdependence of all people, regardless of age, race, class, or nationality.

In 1945, rising from the ashes of World War II, representatives from around the globe met in San Francisco to begin working on a charter for a new international peace organization, the United Nations. Among them was another famous liberal, Franklin Roosevelt's wife, Eleanor. Tireless champion for the poor during her husband's thirteen years as president, she went on to serve as a delegate to the United Nations, chaired its Human Rights Commission, and coauthored the Universal Declaration of Human Rights. For her, the United Nations represented "the greatest hope for a peaceful world. . . . We must use all the knowledge we possess—all the avenues for seeking agreement and international understanding—not only for our own good, but for the good of all human beings."

Both a small and a large "d" Democrat, Eleanor Roosevelt also possessed a liberal Christian temperament. An Episcopalian in the tradition of George Washington, in following Jesus she centered her practical faith on the second great commandment, to love thy neighbor as thyself. "Denominations mean little to me," she said in an interview shortly before she died. "If we pattern our lives on the life of Christ—and sincerely try to follow His creed of compassion and love as expressed in the Sermon on the Mount—we will find that sectarianism means less and less. . . . To me, the way your personal religion makes you live is the only thing that really matters." Her favorite passage in the Bible was I Corinthians 13: "Now abideth faith, hope, charity, these three, but the greatest of these is charity."

Hard-headed pundits argue that one cannot cobble together a program for society on the basis of charity, compassion and neighborliness. They fail to notice one thing. The world is changing. Our founders' ideals, drawn from the scriptures and the laws of nature's God, are less fanciful today than ever before. With the collapse of communism, Eleanor Roosevelt's words are prescient:

> I can never believe any government preserved by fear can stand permanently against a system based on love, trust, and cooperation among its people. Our system, based on love and trust, removes fear so all are free to think and express their ideas, to work and worship as they choose. It is high time that we Americans took a good look at ourselves, . . . remembering how we established a land of freedom and democracy, remembering what we believed in when we did it.

Both Franklin and Eleanor Roosevelt were unashamed of the liberal gospel. Few Americans today possess the same faith. The word *liberal* has shifted in popular parlance from a proud emblem to a hurled epithet representative of everything that is bad about America. Although most scholars, even those critical of liberalism, agree that the American tradition is almost indistinguishable from the liberal tradition, many have lost confidence in the faith of our founders and prophets. From neo-conservatives on the right to liberation theologians on the left, critics argue that the liberal tradition is dysfunctional—economically, morally, and spiritually. From Main Street to the ivory tower, in order to save our country people seem eager to destroy what is most distinctive about it.

The crime varies according to critic: Compassion has run amuck into welfare statism; civil liberty is a cover for all manner of reprehensible and antisocial activity; freedom in a free-market economy means only the freedom to grab. Targeted by critics on both right and left, the word *liberal* has become a catchall for everything that ails us.

Going through the list, a strong superficial case can surely be made, especially by those who couple a liberal value system with the unraveling of society. A fascinating new study, *The Day America Told the Truth*, based on extensive interviews by James Patterson and Peter Kim, indicates a massive breakdown in American morals and values. Their litany is ominous. America has no moral leadership (70 percent of us can't think of a single moral hero). We make up our own moral rules and laws. More than half of us have been victims of a major crime. One of every six Americans has been abused as a child. Date rape is a major, almost wholly unreported epidemic, and a staggering number of girls lose their virginity by the age of thirteen. The United States is by far the most violent industrialized nation on earth; one of seven of us carry a weapon, either on our person or in our car. Most of us will lie, cheat, steal, and worse for a fistful of extra dollars. We lack respect for one another's property. A majority of us malinger, procrastinate, or indulge in substance abuse at work. The list goes on and on. Patterson and Kim conclude, "The United States has become a greedier, meaner, colder, more selfish, and uncaring place. This is no wild inferential speculation, but rather the informed consensus of the American people."

Do liberals share the blame? Of course we do. Individual freedom, the liberty to act as we will, is a bedrock liberal principle. When untethered from responsibility, from our neighbor and the community at large, freedom quickly becomes corrosive, eating away at the foundations of society. This tendency is not limited to today's political and religious liberals, however. It is fed by many free-market moralists and capitalists who have transmuted the original American dream of liberty and justice for all into a vision of glitz powered by greed, a celebration of the pleasures of possessive individualism. Patterson and Kim point out that traditional moral values are less evident in Beverly Hills than in the South Bronx, where only half as many residents use drugs. More importantly, Beverly Hills and the South Bronx have more in common than separates them, at least when it comes to the education of values, because they are equally subject to the powerful allure of televised images that define the good life in terms of goods and not "the good."

So long as we permit, even encourage, a totally free-market approach to everything from wealth accumulation to self-policing of the environment, liberal social engineers, despite their failures, are far less to blame for our current predicament than laissez-faire conservatives and libertarians. As economist Robert Kuttner writes, "Liberals and conservatives agree, in principle, about the value of liberty. But where liberals differ is their insistence that liberty requires greater equality than our society now generates, and that . . . civic society is under assault on a broad front from market society and must be reclaimed if political democracy and a sense of common responsibility are to be part of the American prospect."

If sobering, Patterson and Kim's study of American values contains a number of hopeful indications that we can reclaim civic, and a more civil, society. Most of us are willing to sacrifice to make our country better; we hunger for moral leadership and a new sense of community; and we are profoundly unsatisfied at the direction our country is taking. On the other hand, though we are committed to reintroducing morals and values into the educational system and are deeply worried by the state of American education, "The American 'shopping list' of 'educational' problems sounds more like a prison reform package than a list of educational grievances." And, though we long for it, "There is no meaningful sense of community. Most Americans do not participate in any community action whatsoever."

Here is where a new liberal mandate can reclaim the American spirit and inspire a compelling vision for the restructuring of society. Certainly, the liberal temper or attitude is flexible enough to accommodate a community-centered ethic. Flexible and nondoctrinaire, the liberal mind is able to adapt and change as circumstances change.

Circumstances *have* changed. Today, as Franklin Roosevelt predicted, we are challenged by a new paradigm, far more encompassing than that suggested by White House policy moguls. Its symbol is the shrinking globe. For the first time in history, all who live on mother earth are united in four ways.

We share a common nuclear threat, common environmental threat, global economy, and global communications system. One world is no longer only a vision; it is a reality.

The Chinese have an ideograph for the word *crisis* that might serve as the emblem for our time. It is comprised of two symbols, word-pictures for danger and opportunity. In the crisis we face today, everything we do has global consequence. If the danger is obvious, the opportunity for a new way of living together as kin is equally promising.

One cannot overemphasize the importance of this paradigm shift. Historically, certain basic tenants of liberalism, especially those with ethical connotations, have been dismissed as idealistic. This is true even of the liberalism of Jesus, who taught us to love our enemies and our neighbors as ourselves. Throughout history, the realist could have responded, and often has, with tough-minded and not completely inappropriate derision. For centuries, in political or societal terms, the practical translation of Jesus's saying, "If he asks for your cloak, give him your coat also," might well be, "If you let your enemy have an inch, he will take a mile, and soon your children will be in thralldom to him."

This kind of thinking dominates still. Shortly before his fall, in a *Playboy* interview Donald Trump referred to Mikhail Gorbachev as a wimp, and said of George Bush's favorite aspiration that if we as a nation become any kinder or gentler, we will be a doormat for the entire world.

If anachronistic and unattractive, such opinions are based on solid experience. Competitive virtues such as fortitude were initially not individual but community virtues. Valor in protecting one's family, tribe, or state from enemies across the river or across the world was essential for the survival of one's own people and culture. But when turned into best-selling polemics by people such as Allan Bloom in *The Closing of the American Mind*, this same argument is rendered obsolete by the shift brought about by our shrinking globe. Whether one is speaking of war or the environment, to protect our families we must now struggle to protect our erstwhile enemies' families as well.

The old idealism is therefore the new realism. The new idealist dreams about Star Wars deterrence, indulges in nostalgia for the 1950s, carps about the dangers of letting down our guard, and fights to lower taxes regardless of the long-term cost to society. The new realist is busy painting out the boundaries between peoples, investing in the next generation, caring for the environment and beating swords into plowshares.

The new realist knows that today our own survival depends on our neighbors' survival. In a nuclear age, where global war is murder-suicide or genocide, the only way to win is not to war with one another. With a global environmental threat, none of us has discrete backyards any longer. Every person on this planet is in jeopardy, whether it be us, the Russians, or the Brazilians who are despoiling the environment. And, with the advent of a global economy, we are not strengthened but rather threatened by our neighbors' economic insecurity. For the first time in history, a market crash halfway around the world is like a *tsunami*, a great tidal wave that will surely come crashing down on our own shore.

In response to today's global realities, the old nationalism is beginning to yield to a new ethic, hinted at more than a century ago by Julia Ward Howe, championed by Eleanor Roosevelt, and perhaps best expressed and understood by contemporary feminists. It is a nurturing ethic based on the family model. Competition is replaced by cooperation, and hierarchical structures are supplanted by relational ones. The new ethic has as its cornerstone not the individual, sovereign and free, but rather the community.

In both geopolitical and national terms, to emphasize individual liberties at the expense of social relationships is increasingly dysfunctional. Our own freedom and liberty depend existentially and ontologically on justice being done for and shared with as many others as possible, regardless of faith, politics, or ethnic background. Not that we should sacrifice personal liberty; we should simply modulate it in such a way that our neighbors too are served. We must move from a foundation of atomic individualism to one of community and love.

Untethered to community, liberty becomes wanton. When the rights of criminals are honored above those of victims, when freedom of speech extends to racial epithets and homophobic slurs, when one individual exercises his or her freedom to exploit another, those who defend the individual at the expense of the community become vulnerable to the charge of ethical irresponsibility. To react against people who would impose a single set of values on a pluralistic society is appropriate, but liberalism loses its moral bearings when it places the rights of one individual above those of another. Any insistence on absolute, even abject, freedom for the sovereign individual leads to libertarianism or libertinism, each an idolatrous manifestation of the liberal spirit.

With a global economy, global nuclear and environmental threat, global communications system, and the attendant breakdown of false barriers separating people from one another, today the old *I win/you lose*, tribal or individualistic model is dysfunctional, if not obsolete. A new model, based on the family and therefore especially familiar to women, suggests new metaphors for meaning: the earth as organism, the interdependent web, the kinship of all life. These metaphors are far more faithful to contemporary reality than the old, with God the Father, Lord, and warrior undergirding the patriarchy and invoked by priest and ruler alike to justify the hierarchical structures and competitive systems that sustain it.

In her modern classic, *In a Different Voice*, Carol Gilligan defines community according to an "ethic of care."

> The concept of identity expands to include the experience of interconnection. The moral domain is similarly enlarged by the inclusion of responsibility and care in relationships. And the underlying epistemology correspondingly shifts from the Greek ideal of knowledge as a

> correspondence between mind and form to the biblical conception of knowing as a process of human relationship.

Biblically inspired and family-based, Gilligan's model for community offers a redemptive new metaphor for contemporary liberals. Those who speak in Gilligan's "different voice" form the potential vanguard of a new world, not a brave new world but a more compassionate one. Challenging the rough and tumble lift-yourself-up-by-your-own-bootstrap ethic, they shift our attention from the atomic individual to the community of individuals, people who share common needs that can be fulfilled only through mutual nurture and support. Their symbol is the family.

The weakness of liberal rhetoric on family issues has sprung from two sources. First, we have permitted the far right to define all the terms, thereby ceding the pro-family label. Compounding this error, we have tended to base our counter-arguments on individual rights rather than family needs. If others truncate the family metaphor, reducing it to a cover for moralistic campaigns against women's equality, abortion, pornography, and a secular school system, we run the risk of abandoning it entirely.

Freedom of choice is central to the liberal tradition, but so is neighborly love, the principle that binds us together in redemptive community. Without forsaking various pro-choice options (to have an abortion, follow one's sexual preference in consentual relationships, exercise civil liberty with regard to freedom of speech and religion) today's liberals have an obligation to widen their circle of concern.

Investing value in community is in no way foreign to the liberal tradition. As the Hebrew prophets and such great American liberals as Roger Williams, Thomas Jefferson, and Abraham Lincoln remind us, individual civil liberties are of little worth if not distributed with equity to the greatest possible number.

In the Hebrew scriptures there is no word for individual, only for community, the people. A community is not a group of like-minded people. That is collectivism on a small scale, or individualism writ large. Community is the kinship of all people. To cultivate an ethic based on values such as self-giving, generosity, compassion, tenderness, and mutuality actually extends the liberal spirit to its full compass. As we discover the nature of our interdependencies—that when one suffers we all suffer, that we and our neighbor, even we and our enemy, are truly kin—a new family policy emerges, expanding the comforts of home.

Home can be a conservative metaphor, of course, as in "My home is my castle," that place where families burrow, safe from the foreigner, the other, the outsider. A liberal rendering of home begins with Abraham and Sarah, who open their door and offer hospitality to strangers. Home is not where others are closed out but invited in, a place for companionship, mutuality, communion.

Returning to its root meaning, a companion is one with whom we break bread. We may choose, and often have, to break bread only with those most closely related to us, immediate family and friends. But if we and our neighbor are one, the nature of kinship changes. To bring the comforts of home into the world, to love and feed and serve our neighbor as ourself, transforms the planet into a shared dwelling place. We are attached to one another by what we hold in common, not divided by accidents of birth, whether nationality, sex, color, or economic class.

Having tended hearth and family for so long, women instinctively appreciate this new perspective better than men. Even the stories we tell are different. Educator Sharon Daloz Parks has written, "Men tend to tell and recognize their story primarily in terms that celebrate moments of separation and differentiation. Women tend to tell and recognize their stories in terms of moments of attachment and relation." Though they too may fall into traps of narrowness and exclusion, no group understands or articulates the importance of this better than contemporary feminists.

Expressed in many voices, the feminist ethic stresses two basic shifts: from a competitive to a cooperative value system; and from a hierarchical to a relational social, political, and economic structure. This view of the world may arise from women's experience, but it also addresses contemporary realities with a new set of metaphors.

With good reason, many feminists will have nothing to do with liberalism. Despite the nobility of its rhetoric, along with almost every other system, liberal democracy in the United States has failed to deliver a fair measure of equity to women. This is true of religion also. Countermanding the spirit of the scriptures, Jewish and Christian patriarchy has systematically devalued and oppressed women. Understandably, therefore, many feminists reject Judaism and Christianity, however closely the spirit of their founders and prophets corresponds to the feminist ethic of neighborliness, compassion, and community.

On the other hand, certain expressions of feminist thought cannot be adopted by contemporary liberals. Reversing but not correcting a longstanding wrong, some radical feminists are hesitant to include men in the circle of community. Others claim fidelity to various discredited utopias, whether Arcadian or Marxist. Not that they would wish it, but such postures cannot be fitted to liberal democratic dress.

In each instance, however, these women's anger is understandable and appropriate. The Hebrew prophets were angry too. So was Jesus. This takes nothing away from the truth of their calls for justice or appeals for neighborly love. Until the inequities between male and female, or white and black and brown, are systematically addressed, expressions of anger remain appropriate, even inevitable.

Minorities are oppressed by majorities, even as the powerless are always oppressed, sometimes overtly, but often subtly, even unconsciously, by the powerful. Yet the words of South

African feminist Bernadette Mosala do make one important distinction: "When men are oppressed, it's tragedy. When women are oppressed, it's tradition." If I were Winnie Mandela I would be angry when my husband and Jesse Jackson asked me to take Mrs. Jackson on a tour of the garden, so that they could talk alone, man to man.

For equal work, women today receive 65 cents for every man's dollar as compared to 40 cents one hundred years ago. That is one measure of how far we still have to go, as is the continuing discrimination against African-Americans and Latinos in education and employment. Progress has been made, but the threatened abandonment of liberal social programs, together with the values of neighborliness, liberty with equity, and compassion that inspire them, places a better future in jeopardy. Here contemporary feminist thinkers offer insights that promise to revitalize the liberal tradition by elevating the status of community without diminishing the importance of the individual.

Independent evidence confirms they may be on to something. In Patterson and Kim's study of American values, ranked first in a list of "revelations" is that "Women are morally superior to men."

> This is true all across the country—everywhere, in every single region, on every moral issue we tested. Both sexes say so. Women lie less. Women are more responsible. Women can be trusted more. It is imperative that women be looked to for leadership in America right now in government, in both political parties, in religion, in education, in business.

Whether their high morality rating is related more directly to powerlessness than gender remains an open question. Nonetheless, these findings ratify the claims made by many American feminists. Given the growing impact of women on American politics, religion, and business, they also offer at least a glimmer of hope for the eventual establishment of a more compassionate society. If that is the case, both men and women will benefit. Moving beyond hierarchical power models to relational models stressing nurturance, connectedness, and mutuality, our greatest challenge in America today is to become who we claim to be. Our nation's motto, *E pluribus unum* (out of many, one) is fulfilled only when all the "I's" are also a "we."

This "we" is not an undifferentiated collective; that would ensure the tyranny of the status quo. Minority rights must not only be protected by the majority but cultivated and enhanced for the greater welfare of both. It is not a matter of blending but bringing out all the colors; not of tolerating but respecting other voices and ways.

Here feminism is a handmaiden to something far more encompassing—the spirit of "neighborhood." As an American ideal it is not new. More than half a century ago, when laying the cornerstone for what he called our "good neighbor policy," President Herbert Hoover said that "Democracy is more than a form of political organization; it is a human faith. True democracy is not and cannot be imperialistic. The brotherhood of this faith is the guarantee of good-will."

In 1942, Republican presidential candidate Wendell Wilkie described "the faith that is America" in his book *One World*:

> America must choose one of three courses after this war: narrow nationalism, which inevitably means the ultimate loss of our own liberty; international imperialism, which means the sacrifice of some other nation's liberty; or the creation of a world in which there shall be an equality of opportunity for every race and every nation. I am convinced the American people will choose, by overwhelming majority, the last of these courses. To make this choice effective, we must win not only the war, but also the peace, and we must start winning it now.

President Dwight Eisenhower coupled the American creed with biblical faith in offering this prayer just after being sworn into office in 1952: "We pray that our concern shall be for all the people, regardless of station, race or calling. May cooperation be permitted and be the mutual aim of those who, under the concepts of our Constitution, hold to differing political faiths, so that all may work for the good of our beloved country and Thy glory."

And George Bush calls us to a "kinder and gentler" nation, illumined by "a thousand points of light."

One can always contrast a politician's rhetoric with his or her actions. That takes nothing away from how closely these expressions of the American creed correspond to the new liberal vision for a more cooperative and nurturing value system.

To suggest that such a world could ever be born outside the pages of a book may seem utopian. We have a terrible time living with our neighbors' differences, whether of color, nationality, or faith. But that takes nothing away from the truth, even the practicality of such ideals. If we possess an instinct for survival, such tonics as relationship, nurturance, and mutual respect contain saving power.

Think of it in terms of enlightened self-interest. Once neighborhoods were insulated and prejudices functional for societal bonding. Today we are thrown, in all our glorious and troublesome diversity, into one another's backyards. We can attempt to convert or subdue our neighbors by imposing a dominant set of values, but this form of cultural or religious imperialism invites its own whiplash. As the world shrinks and populations mix, traditional worldviews, whether sponsored by the white men who brought us Western culture or the mullahs who wield the sword of Allah, will only continue to dominate at everyone's peril, including their own. In a pluralistic world, the fundamentalist or idealogue will either go the way of the dinosaur, or bring down himself as he brings down his neighbor. Though our penchant for division, tension, and destruction is manifested daily, if we possess an instinct for survival, over time we shall adapt to these new realities.

Because liberals are better at adapting than almost anyone else, often we are dismissed as lacking backbone or principle.

In fact, the principles we hold most dear are those best suited for these changing times: openness; humility; generosity of spirit; neighborliness; loving compassion toward the other, the stranger, even the enemy.

How we shall achieve this new world order remains unclear. I expect that it will require far more government supervision than during the Reagan and Bush years: much stricter environmental regulation; a real safety net for the impoverished and underprivileged; programs aimed at the protection and cultivation of our children's lives; a more sharply graduated tax code to close the gap between rich and poor; and strict enforcement and protection of all antidiscriminatory legislation.

None of this, however, will restore the necessary sense of community. For that we must build new partnerships, innovative cooperative endeavors between government, private philanthropic and religious institutions, unions, and corporations. We can begin right now with our schools; extend the joint ventures to provide low-cost housing; help to police our neighborhoods with community watch groups; build bridges everywhere across the many divides that estrange us from one another.

Reviving liberal values proves essential today for another reason. The world may be shrinking, but we will never be clones of one another. We can build community only by respecting differences, sometimes major differences. This means educating ourselves in the ways, traditions, and cultures of the other, who lives no longer across the world but right next door. It also means changing the way we live with and listen to one another, not as competing families but as members of a single, fascinating family containing a myriad of hues, customs, and beliefs.

This is not abdication. It is the promised realization of principles on which this liberal democracy was founded, principles inspired by the spirit of the scriptures and read in the text of creation. All are created equal, not alike but equal. All have certain inalienable rights. Among the freedoms we most avidly protect are the freedoms of religion and speech. And the only way to ensure our own liberty is to protect the liberty of our neighbor as well. In a pluralistic world, that means respecting, even honoring differences.

The new liberal gospel is not that different from the old. It impels us to nurture the interdependent web by fostering life and the living system that sustains it; to challenge every power and principality that would divide people from one another on the basis of secondary distinctions, such as race, faith, gender, economic status, or sexual preference; to advance the spirit of universalism while meeting the challenges of pluralism; to counter bigotry, which is the celebration of prejudice; to protect minority rights, opinions, and freedoms, so long as they are not themselves destructive of the commonweal: in short, any cause that enhances human dignity and opens the possibility of ever more inclusive circles of love.

This idealistic vision is today the new realism. Sharon Daloz Parks expresses it as clearly as anyone:

> Might it be useful to develop an imagination in which earth is a home for the dwelling of the whole human family? As cultures now encounter each other in more intimate and threatening ways, might it be useful to recognize that unknown relatives are initially guests to each other, that the art of being a guest is found in the ability to be sensitive to another's space, that the art of being a host is to be found in a sensitivity to the pilgrimage that brought the guest to one's door and to the guest's needs for nourishment and protection? Is not our growing consciousness of pluralism an invitation to recognize more profoundly that we are each guests to the other in the "household of God."

Which truly brings us home to the most famous liberal of them all. Today, God may best be described by organic metaphors, in which the parts, however distinct, cooperate and make up a whole that is greater than all and yet present in each. I think of Paul's body of Christ, one body, many members. The foot and hand and eye each are different, but they need one another, just as we, who differ in faith, race, gender, and ultimate concerns, need one another as well.

Similar metaphors can be drawn from insights in biology, physics, and sociology, which also suggest that the whole is present in each of the parts. To cast this in religious language, the creator is not above and apart from but alive within and shaped by the creation.

One new metaphor for God is the holograph. Shoot two lasers, one off an object and the other directly, through a photoplate consisting of thousands of tiny cells. It will capture a three-dimensional image, recoverable by another laser blast. The wonder is, if you dash the photoplate to bits, even the tiniest shard will still hold, however dimly, a three-dimensional image. Again, the whole is present in each of the parts. This image for God reflects new knowledge and confirms old wisdom. It also offers a divine model—truth writ large—for relationship and interdependence, two foundational concepts for contemporary liberals.

Or think about our bodies, where a colony of cells work together brilliantly, unmindful of their cooperation. However specialized, every cell is signed by the same genetic coding. I wonder. Might we not also, individuals, strangely interdependent with all that lives and breathes on this planet, each contain the DNA of God?

Perhaps the most powerful image suggesting interdependence and the kinship of all life is captured in that picture from space of the earth, blue-green and marbled with clouds, rising over the moon's horizon. This image is reinforced daily, as we become more cognizant of our interdependencies. Each part, every individual, faith, color, and nationality is distinct, but one mother holds us all to her bosom, giving us life, providing us a home.

As Shug says of God in Alice Walker's *The Color Purple*, "My first step away from the old white man was trees. Then air. Then birds. Then other people. But one day when I was sitting quiet and feeling like a motherless child, which I was, it come to me: that feeling of being part of everything, not separate at all."

In America we have a name for this: *E pluribus unum*, out of many, one. It's a liberal epiphany.

# *Epilogue*

I began writing this book two years ago, on June 7, 1989, an auspicious day in the annals of liberal America. On June 7, 1776, Richard Henry Lee, the firebrand of Virginia, sponsored a resolution in the Continental Congress that led to the formation of a committee to draft our Declaration of Independence. And fifty years ago on June 7, the *New York Times* broke its longstanding practice and began capitalizing the word *Negro*, "in recognition of racial self-respect for those who have been for generations 'in the lower case.' "

Ever since 1776, when our founders proclaimed their fidelity to the principles of liberal democracy, we have struggled to preserve and perfect them. Today, people around the globe invoke the same cherished principles in their own struggles for liberation. The day I began writing, China's Tiananmen Square teemed with thousands of students locked in a mortal struggle for freedom of expression, young people inspired by the American experiment, their symbol the Statue of Liberty. In the Soviet Union millions of citizens watched on live television as delegates to the newly elected Congress called openly for expanded democratic and economic reforms, criticized the pace of Glasnost and Perestroika, and condemned Mikhail Gorbachev, the prophet of both, for centralizing too much power in his own office. And, representing perhaps the most dramatic reversal heretofore sanctioned by a communist state, in Poland a two-party election took place, resulting in a stunning mandate for the forces of Solidarity and the communist leaders' offer to form a coalition government.

I finished writing in late April 1991. In the interim, we have witnessed a war in Iraq and an impasse between the forces of democracy and the interests of the establishment in many

Eastern bloc nations. If this represents the new world order, have things changed as much as it had seemed?

I think they have. Whether an invasion was justified or not, the coalition arrayed against Iraq in response to the appropriation of Kuwait was a historic one: multilateral and sanctioned by the United Nations. When a leader such as Saddam Hussein threatens his neighbors it is not a regional or parochial conflict, but one that has international economic and political impact. Since oil powers the engines of the world, anything that jeopardizes supply or anyone who gains disproportionate control over distribution can wreak international havoc. And any leader who seeks to achieve hegemony through wanton military action invites international censure. In the case of Iraq, first by applying economic sanctions and then by approving an armed response, the United Nations acted with greater strength and unanimity than ever before.

Some argue that such crises demonstrate our need to stockpile further armaments and cultivate a healthy suspicion of our neighbors. They miss the point. Vagabond leaders and rogue governments will always bedevil the world. Recalling the body metaphor—one organism with many interdependent parts—international outlaws are part of the world body politic in the same way that a cancerous tumor is; whenever practicable they too must be exised—or, better, isolated and neutralized by an economic tourniquet. How this particular drama played itself out is, in this one respect, secondary. The message implicit in Iraq's adventurism was not that the United States needs to protect itself from its enemies but that the whole world needs to protect itself from its enemies, as long as we remember that, in our preoccupation with our enemies, we may become more like them. Yet, when we recognize our kinship with all people, and act in concert through such bodies as the United Nations to protect our common interest, national differences yield to international shared concerns and Eleanor Roosevelt's dream begins to come true.

As for the continuing struggle behind what was once the

Iron Curtain, it only temporarily muffles and certainly does not smother the cry for liberal democracy. Witness the realignment of Europe over the past two years. In rapid-fire succession communist governments toppled in East Germany, Hungary, Poland, Czechoslavakia, Romania, and Yugoslavia, each replaced by limited yet aspiring liberal democracies. People who once suffered under tyranny now grapple with a new set of problems: how to maintain order, enhance freedom, and establish free-market economies. It is too early to proclaim a new world order, but, in response to international crises, whether sponsored by outlaw nations such as Iraq or brought about by the recognition of global environmental peril, people are working more and more cooperatively together in the United Nations and other international agencies in search of common solutions to shared problems.

Distracted by headlines reflecting chaos and confusion, it is easy to forget how profoundly the world has changed. Focusing on the weakness of our domestic economy and the many divisions within society, how quickly we overlook the principal irony in America today. The liberal spirit is ascendant throughout the world as never before, while languishing in the closet of the country that gave it birth.

The United States of America is a liberal democracy. It is the model for all other liberal democracies. The liberal impulse, both religious and political, shaped our country from its very founding. It informed the development of religious freedom, separation of church and state, democratic institutions and elections, equal protection under the law, freedom of speech and press, and liberal education. Liberal activists led the charge for abolition, spearheaded the union movement, worked for women's suffrage, established social security and Medicare, sponsored the civil rights movement of the 1950s and 1960s, and the women's rights movement of the 1970s and 1980s. The liberal temper assures the ongoing development of pluralism, protection of minorities, respect for subgroups in our society, people with distinct and often unpopular social, religious, political, and sexual identities or viewpoints. When the narrow sympathies of some and the fear of others combine to mute this generous cry, we must give it new voice.

Let me close with an unfashionable word of hope. In the United States today, a possible resurgence of the liberal spirit, especially as adapted to a community agenda, can be detected in our shifting demographics. One generation, the so-called baby boomers, has dictated our national agenda for decades. I am ambivalent about my generation's impact. Heretofore we have contributed more to the problem, than its solution. But we unquestionably weigh heavily in the national balance of social and cultural priorities.

Have you ever watched a boa constrictor eat a baby pig? The snake swallows the pig whole, and the pig goes through the snake an inch at a time, distending it to three times its size. Admitting the all-too-often appropriateness of the metaphor, those of us who were born in the decade and a half following the Second World War are the pig.

When the pig was a child, we lived through the 1950s. Anyone who looks back on the 1950s as boring, the Eisenhower years, forgets how much attention and room had to be given to the young pig. It's no accident that churches have never been fuller, or suburbs more aggressively developed. An enormous amount of energy understandably went into the raising of children, their nurture and education. No surprise here. The baby boomers had begun to set our nation's agenda.

Then came the 1960s. The pig became an adolescent in the 1960s. Healthy adolescents tend to rebel against their parents and all that their parents stand for. The 1960s were a time of unprecedented adolescent rebellion in this country; but, given the disproportionate number of adolescents involved, this is hardly surprising. Many of us took to the street in civil rights and antiwar demonstrations. We were angry. And we were everywhere. Because of our numbers, we changed the face of history. Even my father, who had been arguing against the Vietnam War in the U.S. Senate since 1963, admitted that had it not been for the massive disruption of society caused by the student protests, Lyndon Johnson would not have stepped down from the presidency, and the war would not have ended as soon as it did.

The 1970s followed. It was the "me" decade, which, again, is hardly a surprise. We baby boomers were young adults, in our twenties, establishing careers, making connections, finding mates, purchasing as many grown-up toys as possible. For better and for worse, the pig had negotiated the passage from adolescent rebellion to pragmatic narcissism.

Then came the eighties. Now in our thirties, many of us had achieved a fair measure of material success, struggled with our personal relationships, and gotten bored with our toys. Parents die; friends begin to die. Mortality invades our consciousness. Finally, the pig has to face the facts. It is growing up. So what does it do? It launches on a search for meaning.

Which leads us to the nineties. By 1996, the average baby boomer will be over forty. If married, he or she likely will have a young family—the baby boomlet. With new responsibilities, the pig begins looking for meaningful connections.

This potentially is the good news. Inspired by a renewed sense of responsibility, and awakened by nostalgia for its heyday in the sixties, the pig may begin to discover values more abiding than its own little piggy-bank of pleasures. If too old to take to the streets, it finally may be old enough to care for its neighbor as itself. Among other things, for the first time in a long while it considers returning to synagogue or church.

My parable is a stretch, even for a liberal like me who far too often commits the sin of optimism. But if it pans out, the coming decade may in fact become the "we" decade, inaugurating a new era of community, interdependence, cooperation, and commitment to the commonweal.

This dream may prove naive. And I know how fashionable it is to put down dreamers. That has always been the fate of liberals. We believe in the future, and try to make it better than the present. And sometimes we fail. Yet, to quote my liberal mother, "Though in my personal attempts to advance a more compassionate vision, as in anyone's, I'll often be wrong (though my temptation, being human, is to say occasionally wrong), I'll continue to try to affect people's lives for the better, remembering that we are living in one world, full of people who are different but in a larger sense the same, each a child of God."

In a nutshell, that is the liberal gospel.

# Index